Rural Housing and the Public Sector

DAVID R. PHILLIPS
and
ALLAN M. WILLIAMS
University of Exeter

Gower

Published by Gower Publishing Company Limited,
Gower House, Croft Road, Aldershot, Hampshire,
GU11 3HR, England

British Library Cataloguing in Publication Data

Phillips, David R.
  Rural housing and the public sector.
  1. Public housing-England 2. Housing
  management-England
  I. Title II. Williams, Allan M.
  352.7'5   HD7334.A3

  ISBN 0-566-00456-9

Reproduced from copy supplied
printed and bound in Great Britain
by Billing and Sons Limited and Kemp Hall Bindery
Guildford, London, Oxford, Worcester.

Contents

Preface

The research upon which this book is based commenced in 1979. At that time we had prepared an outline of our intended research into rural local authority housing, and were looking for a suitable case study area in the South West of England as a generally 'rural' region. It was largely fortuitous that we chose South Hams, despite its many interesting socio-economic and housing features. Through our activities in the South West Branch of the Regional Studies Association, we came into contact with Gerard Heywood who, as well as being Branch Chairman, is also a councillor with the South Hams District Council. We discussed our proposal with him and he considered it to be of sufficient interest to the Council to put us in contact with Mr Douglas Macfarlane, the Chief Housing Officer for the area.

Thereafter, progress was rapid: in consultation with Mr Macfarlane and his Deputy, Mr David Ashman, a research proposal was finalised which aimed to cover both our academic interests and the authority's need for basic information concerning local authority housing in South Hams. The South Hams District Council then agreed to support a research assistant for six months, and Mr Geoffrey Brown was appointed from October 1979. In all this we were very fortunate. In the South Hams we found housing officers and local councillors with the flexibility of outlook to enable them to allow access to their records to outsiders, and with the willingness to finance a rare example of co-operation between academics and administrators, while in Geoff Brown we found an exceptional research assistant. He undertook the major task of collating and coding an enormous amount of data and also provided the imaginative insight to uncover a number of obscure sources of information. From the initial analysis, a series of five working papers was produced for the District Council and details of the data sources and methodologies used for these are given in Appendix A. To all these persons, and also to many others in the Housing and Planning Departments of South Hams District Council, we are grateful for invaluable help.

A number of other persons have provided us with support within the University of Exeter itself. The project required a large number of illustrations and these were expertly provided by Mr Rodney Fry's Cartographic Unit within the Geography Department; Mr Chris Mann, in particular, did a considerable amount of work on the maps. Essential support was also provided by Mr Andrew Teed, the Department's photographic technician, who prepared the diagrams for publication. In addition we were also able to draw on the advice of our colleagues Dr Mark Blacksell and Mr Andrew Gilg, who kindly read and commented on our manuscript. We also gratefully acknowledge the assistance of the University of Exeter Research Fund which provided us with a grant towards the cost of preparing the final manuscript for publication. This was expertly typed by Mrs Lyn Longridge.

Finally, it is important to state that, although the research project was a joint venture, this work as it stands and its conclusions are based upon our own academic judgment and do not necessarily coincide with the views of South Hams District Council. Furthermore, the responsibility for any errors, omissions and vagaries of interpretation of data which we may have made remains ours alone.

D.R.P.
A.M.W.
Department of Geography
University of Exeter

1 Introduction

A number of writers have drawn attention to the general paucity of research on the social problems of rural areas, implying that there has been an over-concentration on urban affairs. As recently as 1978, Walker (1978a, p.1) edited a book on rural poverty, the main aim of which was ".... to begin to counter the predominantly urban image of poverty and deprivation ...." and the ".... increasing tendency for planners of transport, recreation, social services and other provisions to ignore the problems of those people living on low incomes outside or on the periphery of large population settlements".

Several reasons are usually suggested to explain this apparent neglect of rural areas. On the one hand, Shaw (1979b, p.189) emphasises that ".... the image of poverty is an urban image ...." and that this is partly because ".... rural problems, particularly those relating to low levels of access of opportunities, tend to be less visible than urban squalor". This is certainly true of the media who consistently focus on the more sensational aspects of urban crises, whether these be physical obsolescence, increasing crime rates or inner city unemployment. It is also true of government sponsored research, as illustrated by the attention given in the 1970s to the Community Development Projects and the Department of the Environment's inner city studies. In contrast to this perception of urban problems, rural areas are seen through ".... the public stereotype of the peaceful, caring village community, providing inter-familial support in true Archers' style ...." (Walker 1978a, p.10). The problems of rural areas are dismissed, either on the grounds of there being no really rural areas, so they can only be suffering from the consequences of urban problems, or as being negligible when compared with the scale of urban problems. Neither of these formulations is correct as recent studies of poverty, deprivation and accessibility have gone some way to show (Moseley 1978; Walker 1978b; Moseley 1979; Shaw 1979a).

It can be argued that the conceptual separation of urban and rural problems implies an unrealistic dichotomy, concentrating on the superficial symptoms of the social and economic problems of these areas, whilst neglecting the underlying root causes in the changing political economy of the UK. The spirit of this argument can easily be accepted; for example, unemployment and low incomes in rural areas are obviously not the outcome of a unique set of 'rural forces', but stem from the capitalist development of Britain (see Campbell 1981). Nevertheless, it is still important to study rural areas in their own right for three reasons. First, the costs of service provision in rural areas are usually higher than in urban areas (Heller 1978) so that the levels of provision may be lower and more spatially concentrated (to achieve economies of scale), hence exacerbating inherent problems of accessibility. Secondly, the struggle over political control of local government has had a distinctive outcome in rural areas. Rose et al (1978, p.15) state that ".... in rural areas such as East Anglia, landowners are not simply well represented on local councils but are consistently able to define key issues in ways which tend to further their sectional interests to the detriment of working class groups ....". As Newby et al (1978) have shown, this is most clearly evident in the realm of housing, with local authority provision being minimised so as to maximise the control functions of tied accommodation and to minimise financial burdens on ratepaying landowners. Finally, even though rural problems may appear to be similar to those of urban areas, they frequently require special remedial policies, such as the provision of mobile services and 'irregular' public transport (Moseley 1979).

It is for reasons such as these that the neglect of rural problems is of serious concern. However, to speak of a total neglect of rural problems is rather misleading. More accurately, interest in rural areas is cyclical, and this applies both to the level of research and the aspects of the rural problems being studied. Lewis (1981) has indicated some of the major stages in the cycle of post-war research on rural communities. In the 1940s, the distinctiveness of the rural way of life was a major theme; in the 1950s, attention switched to the depopulation of rural areas, and, in the 1960s (accompanying a reverse in population trends), the metropolitan village and the rural-urban fringe became the foci of interests.

More recently, research has followed (if belatedly) trends in other spheres of the social sciences, to examine the social and welfare problems of rural inhabitants. Cloke (1980a, p.190) sees this as a major change, because the traditional interests of rural social research have ".... revolved around migration, depopulation and community structure". As part of the new emphasis, studies have been published on such themes as transport and accessibility (Moseley 1979), recreation (Patmore 1970), deprivation (Shaw 1979b), planning the countryside (Gilg 1978), structure planning (Shaw and Williams 1980), rural incomes (Thomas and Winyard 1979), health services (Heller 1979), education (Watkins 1979) and social services (Stockford 1978). However, this impressive range of studies represents only a start and actually helps to identify other gaps, so that Cloke (1980a, p.181) has recently stated that there is ".... a widespread awareness of the deficiencies of rural geography and planning ....".

The deficiency is as much one of methodology as one of substantive knowledge. Although the amount of research into rural areas has increased considerably in very recent years, many writers consider that there is still a methodological gap between urban and rural investigations. This is implied by Cloke (1980a p.182) when he suggests that ".... there now exists a substantial body of descriptive and, to a lesser extent, explanatory literature directed towards the rural environment". More directly, Moseley (1980), commenting on rural deprivation research, states that the focus has been almost entirely on the 'consumers' rather than on the producers of deprivation. Furthermore, he considers that a comparison of rural and urban geography (as an example of a subject with a major interest in rural matters) is instructive in highlighting methodological weaknesses in the former. Following Robson (1979), he writes that studies of urban geography in the 1970s can be seen as progressing through four overlapping phases. These are (i) quantitative model building, (ii) behaviouralism, (iii) managerialism, and (iv) political economy. In contrast, Moseley (1980, p.97) feels that rural geography has become 'bogged down' in the first two of these stages. It is still focusing on the sufferers of deprivation rather than on the managers of rural resources or on the political and economic features that create this deprivation.

Most rural studies are still concerned with quantitative model building (Cloke 1978; Thomas and Winyard 1979; Ventris 1979) or with the behavioural approach (Clark and Unwin 1979; Haynes et al 1978; Hill 1978). There are relatively few studies of the rural managers although there are important exceptions (Heller 1978; Newby et al 1978) and no substantial contribution in the realm of the political economy approach.

Research on rural housing, which is the concern of this book, has followed a similar pattern. There has been a general neglect of rural housing issues, as a survey of the contents of any of the standard books on housing would reveal (Cullingworth 1966; Nevitt 1966; Donnison 1967).

Larkin (1978c, p.40) considers that

"A major reason for the neglect of rural housing policy is the fact that housing problems in rural areas are not as clearly identifiable, nor so concentrated as is the case in the inner cities. By definition, the countryside does not contain street after street of decaying, overcrowded houses. Yet there is no doubt that major housing problems, such as overcrowding, sub-standard property, and lack of security, do exist in rural areas, and on occasions exist to a proportionally greater extent than in some urban parts."

Most of the earlier work focused attention on the physical condition of rural housing (see chapter three) and only belatedly has there been an awareness that the real problems may be those related to social and economic access to housing. Rogers (1976) has conducted important work in this reorientation and, since his useful review in the mid-1970s, a number of studies of rural housing has been published. Dunn et al (1981) have drawn attention to the relative advantages and disadvantages of different tenure groups. In an analysis of two case study areas, the Cotswold and South Oxfordshire districts, they use quantitative methods to describe the social characteristics of different tenure groups and to relate these to housing opportunities in order to identify deprivation in rural housing. Questionnaire surveys were also used to provide information on movement through the housing stock so as to establish the main features of 'movers' and 'stayers'. Although they also pay some attention to the managers of rural housing, in essence their study represents the most thorough example that is available in rural housing research of quantitative model building and behaviouralism. As such, this study provides invaluable description rather than the explanation which has been called for by Cloke (1980a) and Moseley (1980).

The analysis of managerial control over access to rural housing represents the next approach. This approach derives its clearest formulation from the work of Pahl (1970), which will be discussed more fully in chapter three. Essentially, this seeks to explain access to resources (including housing) through a study of the local decision makers or gatekeepers; in housing, these include the local authority housing officers and councillors, building society managers and estate agents. A number of recent writers have at least partially adopted this approach. Niner (1975) has made a comparative study of housing management practices in different local authorities; Larkin (1978b) has examined the development of council housing in rural areas; Newby et al (1978) considered the relationship between housing development and local political control; and, most recently, Shucksmith (1981) has analysed local government intervention in housing in the Lake District.

All these studies have made valuable contributions, but it is still true to say that far less is known about the managers of rural housing than their urban counterparts; this applies across the board to all managerial participants in the housing market, whether local authority housing managers (see Gray 1976a), estate agents (see Williams 1976), building societies (see Boddy 1980) or landlords (see Rex and Moore 1967). The aim of this book is to extend our knowledge in respect of one of these groups of managers, namely those in the local authority sector. The structure of the book follows on from this objective. In Section A, social change and housing in rural Britain are reviewed and this identifies some of the key problems of housing stress and accessibility. It is suggested that, for the rural poor, local authority housing provides the most likely means by which they can improve both their standards of accommodation and their access to employment, services and social activities. In order to evaluate the actual role of the local authority, a case study approach is adopted, so Section B outlines the context of rural housing in South Hams, a district in South Devon. Section C then provides an analysis and evaluation of housing need and housing management policies in this district, leading onto the final section which considers the policy implications of the study. Methodological details are then provided in Appendix A. The importance and, incidentally, the timeliness of such a study is highlighted by the comments with which Dunn et al (1981, p.255) end their study:

"A cardinal feature of the social limits to growth is the fact that those who are in the vanguard of social change gain most and those who come late gain least. In the realm of rural housing this study has shown that the pecking

4

order has already been clearly drawn. It is the essential role of social policy to ensure that those who come late are at least assured of a reasonable deal."

The most potent social policy available to local authorities lies in the utilisation of their own public housing resources. It is this role that will be under review here. This book, then, is firmly located within the managerialist approach, the third of those considered by Moseley. The fourth of the approaches, political economy, would enquire how 'the pecking order' was determined rather than how social policy can be formulated to remedy its housing implications. Future work which tries to extend our understanding of rural housing will have to consider this approach. Meanwhile, there are still important gaps in our knowledge of the activities, aims and objectives of rural managers involved in housing, and it may be hoped that this research will help to fill a few of these.

SECTION A

HOUSING IN RURAL BRITAIN

2 Social change in rural areas

CHANGE IN THE VILLAGE

Change in the village is a major theme in much contemporary geographical and sociological writing (Woodruffe 1976; Moseley 1979; Newby 1979; Glyn-Jones 1979; Blacksell and Gilg 1981; Dunn et al 1981). 'Change' can be something as measurable and quantifiable as population shifts or something much more subtle such as altering attitudes or modifications to rural access- ibility. More fundamentally, this 'change' may stem from alter- ations in the functions of particular areas in the national economy.

However, for the purposes of this book, it is convenient to commence this review with one of the more pervasive aspects of change, which concerns the changing types of people living and working in rural areas. This is not the place to enter into details about the modernisation of British agriculture and its increased labour productivity, which have led to there being a much smaller 'traditional' rural employment base today; these topics are fully covered elsewhere (see, for instance, Deane 1965; Chambers and Mingay 1966; Jones 1973; Beresford 1975). Traditionally, however, even if members of the village were not working directly on the land as farmers or labourers, they were involved in occupations closely allied to farming such as blacksmiths, millers and other crafts and agricultural services. Hence, due to the dependence largely upon a single industry, it is possible to speak of the village community in late nineteenth century Britain as an 'occupational community' (Newby 1979). However, these conditions have been altering. Agricultural jobs have been in decline and social and economic changes in employment and housing have led to many new social groups becoming involved in the life of rural areas; therefore, the village can no longer be regarded as a closed, occupational community with common ties, aims and objectives. Changes of many types can be introduced either by newcomers to the rural scene or by returned migrants who have worked at home or abroad. The changing social composition of rural areas can apparently affect the very process of change in all aspects of rural life - in technology, social aspirations, employment and recreation.

A number of important statements are to be found concerning this changing composition of rural population in Britain, not only in demographic terms (such as age structure or numbers) but also in social terms (the types of people living in rural locations). The shifting balances of social groups can thus be of great importance to life in any area but this is particularly so in smaller rural settlements. It is useful to refer to an early classification of groupings in rural society (Stamp 1949).

9

In this, three main categories of people are recognised:

(a) The 'Primary Rural Population', such as farmers, farm workers and foresters, depending directly on the land for their livelihood.

(b) The 'Secondary Rural Population', which exists to serve the primary population and so completes the essential composition of the 'occupational community'. Village shop-keepers, smiths, wheelwrights, and village services such as doctor, schoolteacher, vet, parson and publican are given as examples by Stamp.

(c) The 'Adventitious Population', who live in the countryside by choice. Many of these have retired from the active occupations of the first two categories, whilst others may prefer rural surroundings in which to live, whilst they work (or have worked) in nearby towns. This group in particular can be envisaged as potentially being outside the 'occupational community', as they look elsewhere to find their employment and incomes.

As Saville (1957) points out, these groupings form useful categorisations but are by no means precise and, indeed, a large proportion of the secondary rural service population is to be found not only in local market towns but, even further removed, in larger urban centres. This is increasingly true as larger catchment threshold populations become the norm for certain types of service functions. There are also those who live in rural areas and work in towns not through choice, but because they are so constrained by the housing market, as is explained later.

Newby (1979) suggests that there has been the almost total disappearance of the English lowland village as an occupational community and sees a useful distinction instead between 'locals' and 'newcomers'. "There are now few villages without their complement of newcomers who work in towns. These new immigrants have brought with them an urban middle-class lifestyle which is largely alien to the remaining agricultural population ...." (Newby 1979, p.165). This duality can be divisive in that newcomers do not make the village a focus of all their social activities. The possession of a car enables them to maintain social contacts with friends elsewhere and, if necessary, to utilise urban amenities whilst living in the countryside. This dual grouping, with different social circles, frequently different financial circumstances and, as a result, differential mobilities and aspirations, can create and exacerbate the rural problems, which are more fully discussed in the following section.

Pahl (1968, 1970) distinguishes, even more explicitly, various sub-groupings of the rural population who are particularly likely to be found in the rural-urban fringe 'metropolitan village'. He identifies six groupings in his 1968 paper and eight in his 1970 work. In the latter, the following are outlined: large property owners, salaried immigrants with some capital (a salariate of business and professional people), spiralists (who move a number of times to further their careers), urban workers with little capital and little income (often forced out of town, to become reluctant commuters), the retired (of various backgrounds), council house tenants (who frequently have to find work elsewhere rather than in their immediate village), tied cottages and other tenants (the rural poor, with low wages and poor housing) and, finally, local tradesmen and owners of small businesses. To this classification of more or less permanent rural dwellers can be added a further grouping of second home owners, intermittently resident in their rural homes, and increasingly recognised as an important sub-group (Bielckus et al 1972; Coppock 1977; Sarre 1981). The relative positions of some of these main groups in the rural housing market is discussed in general in chapter three and, in the case of Devon, in chapter four. It seems that the different, and sometimes competing, housing needs of these groups can lead to varying levels of 'social justice' in rural housing and this theme is returned to later.

Pahl (1970, p.60) suggests that ".... there is no village population as such; rather there are specific populations which for various, but identifiable, reasons find themselves in a village ....". It is misleading to consider that 'the village' is a sort of average of all the groups suggested above. Some of the groups choose to move from the town to live in a village, some have property in the country (the main or a second home) but choose to spend more time in the city. Others are obliged or constrained to live in the country although they work in towns (the reluctant commuters). On the other hand, however, some sectors of the village society have no choice but to live locally, either in accommodation tied to their work, or because low rural incomes or the lack of occupational skills prevent them from living or working elsewhere. The warning by Frankenberg (1969, p.238) is of relevance: ".... all communities are societies but not all societies are communities ....". The process of change may be creating a variety of communities in social and spatial terms.

Additional evidence for the existence of different social groups in rural areas is given by Ambrose (1974). His groupings take into account not only tenure and income, but also the important aspects of mobility and accessibility (through the availability of private transportation in the face of declining public transport provision). Ambrose's groupings are as follows:

1. Those with capital, able to afford a 'character house' and run two cars
2. Those who can afford a four-bedroom house and run a car
3. Those who can afford a two- or three-bedroom semi and can run a car
4. People in similar circumstances but who cannot run a car
5. Those unable to purchase but who are able to obtain a council house and to afford a car
6. People in similar circumstances but who cannot run a car
7. Those unable to purchase, unable to obtain a council house and who live in privately rented accommodation

11

In this classification, the possession of a car is of direct relevance because, as will be discussed later, it allows access to numerous service and employment opportunities which would otherwise be more restricted. A corollary of this is that, naturally, it also permits a considerable degree of flexibility in residential location. Dunn et al (1981) feel that these groupings have great importance in questions of rural housing, and it should be borne in mind that Pahl was also suggesting that his typology of rural social groupings was of specific applicability to housing policy.

The existence of these various social groups (however defined) implies that there are identifiable interest groups, all of which are important to the changing nature of rural society. Some act as agents of innovation - newcomers, returned migrants, various professional persons; others may, in fact, act to maintain existing practices and power bases. Newby et al (1978) suggest that, although there has been a marked decline this century of the dominance of the squirearchy (an easily identifiable rural ruling class), their power has by no means disappeared. Indeed, it may be argued that it has merely reappeared in a quasi-official context, as the same social stratum may dominate local councils and, hence, very strongly influence local planning decisions with inevitable economic and social consequences. A small number of well-organised individuals in key strategic positions in local institutions ".... may regularly dominate a relatively disorganised majority ...." (Newby et al 1978, p.228).

In terms of access to employment, services and housing, important local figures may be able to exercise strict control. Therefore, the concepts of urban 'managerialism' and 'gatekeeping' (discussed more fully in chapter three) can be applied in rural settings, although with some reservations. Councillors and key council officials may act as gatekeepers to scarce resources such as local authority housing. Nevertheless, it does not necessarily follow that if farmers (or any other powerful groups) occupy gatekeepers' positions, they are as a result powerful. Power is a potential quality; political positions represent only one type of power resource but one which may give control of local circumstances and resource allocations (Newby et al 1978). However, these contentions are of importance in the context of this book, as Newby et al (1978) argue that a number of ploys exist through which the power of the farming lobby is maintained. For example, low rates of local authority housing provision can be justified to keep the rates down, and planning refusals for industrial estates are justified on landscape preservation grounds whilst, in reality, both of these perpetuate a low wage rural economy and the tied cottage system (Gilg 1980a). Farming incomes and control over tenants may thereby be upheld. Certain newcomers may also become collaborators in these tactics, trying to exclude what they consider to be inappropriate and intrusive development, whilst actually supporting the farmers' or landowners' position.

At the same time, newcomers may themselves be the unwitting

purveyors or agents of change. Newcomers are not necessarily a part of the rural scene; they do not always make use of local facilities and services, being mobile enough to use facilities elsewhere. Only infrequently will they be directly dependent upon the rural economy for their income and they will not as a rule bring extra employment opportunities to the area, being essentially self-sufficient. Possibly, extra schools and welfare services will be required eventually to serve their needs but, frequently, they have wider horizons than locals, and can be a generally disquieting element in rural society. If the settlement in which they take up residence is expanded solely to meet their requirements, then their effects may not be undesirable. As it seems likely that, in the future, the only large movements of outsiders will be into rural settlements designated for expansion (as discussed later), then their wider influence may be dissipated. However, the smaller settlements, where even a small proportion of outsiders can significantly influence the composition and attitudes of inhabitants, are often the most vulnerable.

The study of rural social structure has become a major theme in rural social research and is often reflected in the numerous sociological community studies preceding the work by Pahl (such as those by Williams 1956; Stacey 1960; Littlejohn 1964 and Ambrose 1974) and these have been very adequately reviewed elsewhere (Frankenberg 1966; Jones 1973; Lewis 1979; Newby 1979). These community studies have often been stimulated by a tacit recognition of changing economic and social circumstances in the countryside and their effects in local areas. However, bedevilled by the romanticism which tends to be associated with most descriptions of the English countryside, a rigorous assessment of the social well-being and the social and economic conditions of rural Britain has hardly developed (Shaw 1979a). The same can be said of analysis of change in rural areas, since few studies adequately analyse the reasons for, and mechanisms of, change in rural Britain. The nature, location and allocation of rural housing is of major importance in the process of change although, to date, these aspects have received relatively little detailed research attention.

POPULATION CHANGE AND SETTLEMENT POLICIES

One final aspect of change in rural areas, the changing emphasis of rural settlement policies, requires mention before analysing specific rural problems. Until the 1930s, rural areas were gradually losing population to urban areas, but the post-war period has seen a reversal of this trend and the proportion of people living in administratively defined rural areas has progressively increased from 18.7 per cent in 1951 to 19.4 per cent in 1961 and to 21.7 per cent in 1971. Certain of the 'truly rural' remote upland areas and a few lowland agricultural areas have still declined (with population losses as high as 15 per cent between 1951 and 1971), but the majority of rural areas have gained population. During the decade to 1971, the total population of rural areas in England and Wales increased

13

by 18.3 per cent compared to an increase of only 5.8 per cent in the country as a whole (Department of the Environment 1977).

Woodruffe (1976), Moseley (1979) and others echo these suggestions that there is need to dispel the myth that rural depopulation is the norm in Britain. Basically, the picture has been one of net population decline in remoter areas because of economic changes, with lowland England largely offsetting this decline through the in-migration of retired people and of economically active commuters to urban areas. In addition, the suburbanisation and decentralisation of employment (Department of the Environment 1976) has frequently resulted in rather longer car-borne rural commuting journeys being made by many employees, as opposed to suburban commuting to city centres by public transport.

It is certain that the twofold division, into depopulation in remote areas and expansion in the accessible countryside, is simplistic and especially limited in explaining variations at the local level (Dunn et al 1981). Whilst certain rural areas may gain or lose population, there have been some distinct readjustments within localities. Particular settlements, favoured in terms of service and transport provision, have often gained population markedly in recent years whilst other nearby villages have steadily lost population and have become further downgraded. These trends are adequately to be seen in Devon, in chapter four. In addition, the age structure of some rural populations can become distinctly elderly due to out-migration of the young and in-migration of retired persons. Many rural areas now have 30 per cent or more of their population over retirement age as opposed to the national average of 17 per cent, and many of these people may later become frail and dependent upon poor or non-existent rural social services.

Within rural areas, population distribution has been influenced by changing settlement policies. "The main feature is that population growth has tended to correlate positively with proximity to larger urban centres ...." (Moseley 1979, p.12). This has been fostered, at least in part, by the concentration of services into designated favoured locations in key settlement policies. Cloke (1979, 1980a, 1980b, 1980c) reviews these policies, pointing out that the needs of countryside planners have largely been to cope with decline in remote rural areas or growth in the highly pressurised areas within the orbit of larger urban settlements.

The key settlement has, somewhat surprisingly, been viewed by many planners as ".... the universal elixir for multiple rural ailments ...." (Cloke 1979, p.22). The policy has the fundamental objective of concentrating rural resources into selected centres. Certain discrepancies of terminology exist as to the precise meaning of 'key settlements' but, specifically, key settlements form not only major foci for housing, services and employment but also have special functional relationships with the other settlements. In particular, concentration of residential development into certain selected centres enables economies of scale to be derived, and also protects from excessive residential pressure, settlements where further large scale growth would be environmentally inappropriate. Key settlements would thus channel growth into settlements considered to be environmentally and socially capable of undergoing expansion. In remoter areas, they can act as centres for service provision and the promotion of growth, where these would not otherwise be viable. As such, it may be the objective to contain migration to mostly internal rural movement to key settlements, rather than contributing to overall population loss.

Recently, considerable debate has revolved around the relative merits of concentration versus dispersal policies for rural settlements. The key settlement approach has been used from time to time in many counties in Britain, such as Cambridgeshire, Devon and Warwickshire (Cloke 1979). However, some observers suggest this creates unbalanced rural communities in which urban-based planning standards will eventually lead to urban-type problems in rural settlements. Cloke (1979, 1980a) draws three conclusions on key settlement policies in Britain, suggesting that criticisms of the strategies are often based more on their implementation than on inherent qualities of the policy itself; that rural social scientists tend to lack techniques of policy evaluation with which to compare alternatives; and, finally, that the choice between one key settlement and growth of a few smaller settlements tends to be academic anyway, since the major rural social problems are often found in villages well beyond the sphere of influence of any potential growth centre. On the whole, these seem to be very fair comments.

Nevertheless, the debate concerning concentration versus dispersal in rural settlement policies will undoubtedly continue in Britain and elsewhere. The concentration of services and jobs into key settlements has a major implication for housing, because it is most likely that, only within settlements so designated, will major residential development be permitted. Villages which are not selected have usually seen little development, and have thus increasingly appeared as satellite settlements looking to their nearest key village for basic facilities and services (Dunn et al 1981). Such restrictive policies can effectively fossilise non-key villages in their present form with very little new housing provided in them, apart from some minor infilling. Therefore, the influence of the local authority can become very important, both in the role of planning authority and as provider of council housing which is liable to be permitted only in key settlements, especially with the current curtailment of local authority expenditure. In effect, the flexibility of providing homes where needed and for the appropriate social groups can be lost. This is important because new private housing development in many villages has tended to be of an 'up-market', expensive type. This is not necessarily the direct result of key settlement policy, although the policy naturally has the effect of focusing and restricting more general development.

Underlying this debate is the recognition that rural areas do suffer from many economic and social problems, which may be modified, exacerbated or even caused by settlement policies.

These problems may not be uniquely 'rural', but they are certainly in evidence even if not as starkly visible as in some urban settings, and this theme is developed in the following sections.

PROBLEMS IN RURAL AREAS

Recent attention has focused on the identification of social and economic features of rural areas although this has often not been matched by a systematic appraisal of the type and the extent of problems faced by many of them. The work of Shaw (1979a) illustrates the increasingly sophisticated analysis of rural problems, and the expansion from a few foci of research (such as land resources, rural depopulation and community studies) to include general aspects of accessibility and deprivation. A broader dimension of research activity is clearly involved in this approach, which invites consideration of the themes of welfare, social justice, managerialism and allocative justice, previously largely studied only in urban settings. These concepts are discussed further at the end of this chapter and are developed in the later empirical chapters.

Accessibility

Within the 'deprivation jigsaw', as Cloke (1980a) calls it, and the much-cited decline of rural services, a major issue is that of accessibility. Accessibility to employment, to a range of services, to housing, to friends and relatives, and to entertainment, all impinge very directly upon the quality of life enjoyed by rural inhabitants. Accessibility has, of course, at least two major aspects, the socio-economic (for example, do residents feel able to use a service and can they afford to use it?) and locational (that transport is available to reach the service or that it is within easy walking distance). To continue the example of service provision, certain services have greater distance decay factors than others, particularly in the convenience goods or convenience services category, as compared with specialist goods or services. In terms of central place theory, the 'ranges' of goods or services vary, which can mean that, for certain services, very large catchment areas will have to be covered in rural areas to include sufficient consumers. Therefore, only a few locations may be able to support these services, which will inevitably lead to problems of accessibility for some sections of their served populations. The three main reviews of rural deprivation and social issues all identify the general problem of accessibility and attach it to specific services (Moseley 1978; Walker 1978b; Shaw 1979a). In particular, it is argued that poor accessibility will tend to lead to a difference between the aspirations and desires of some rural residents (especially the young) and the local realities. This has been illustrated for employment opportunities in particular, by Shaw and Toyne (1978).

In response to the locational aspects of accessibility problems, there tend to be higher rates of car ownership even though *per capita* incomes are relatively lower than in urban areas. Nationally, in 1976, 56 per cent of households owned a car, with this figure typically being 10 to 20 per cent higher in rural areas. This still means that, in Britain, one-quarter to one-third of all rural households lack a car and, while national car ownership rates may still rise, saturation level must almost have been reached in many rural areas, especially those with high proportions of elderly residents (Moseley 1979). A substantial proportion of people will therefore depend upon public transport, which is declining in frequency and increasing in expense to users. In addition, long rural distances by car become increasingly costly for individuals and families as success-ive British governments regard tax increases on petrol as a reliable source of revenue. Moseley (1979) still feels that the marginal cost of rural motoring is relatively low, yet in terms of low rural wages and rising proportions of the elderly, there are substantial numbers of rural residents in some of the less privileged groups, identified by Pahl and Ambrose, who find accessibility a major problem.

In their survey of two rural areas in lowland Britain, Dunn et al (1981) used car-ownership as a surrogate indicator for assessing accessibility. The proportions of local authority housing respondents with no car were 19 per cent (Cotswold District) and 25 per cent (South Oxfordshire), whilst the proportions of respondents with no car in 'poor housing' were 29 per cent and 32 per cent respectively. This seems to confirm the contention that significant groups of rural residents are without personal transport, but the study also found surprisingly high rates of two-car families (even in local authority housing). In this case, it could be suggested that considerable sacrifices are being made by rural residents to maintain their mobility out of sheer necessity, possibly due to the inadequacy of public transport provision.

Moseley poses the alternatives available to a village which loses its bus service. The car-less residents have three basic choices: to migrate (a drastic step), to make alternative transport arrangements or to increase their village-based activities. The latter two options might, of course, not be possible and the first may be socially and economically undesirable. The results of such an occurrence as the loss of a bus service could be to alter fundamentally the social basis of the village. If migration did occur on a large scale, this might merely make room for larger proportions of adventitious population or second home owners. This simple example does illustrate the vulnerability of certain rural sectors to changing transport provision, possibly at the whim of public bodies.

Apart from the general locational features of accessibility in rural areas which, it should be emphasised, affect very differently the various subgroups of the rural population, certain major themes are constantly in evidence in the literature. This is not the place for a full review of rural deprivation or 'social problems', but the listing below provides a useful backcloth against which housing provision and housing need can be assessed.

Broadly, the following issues can be discerned:

1. Economic opportunities
   Low rural incomes
   Access to jobs and rural unemployment

2. Access to service opportunities
   Health services
   Welfare and social services
   Education
   Community and welfare rights information

3. Access to housing

Poor access to housing is separately considered, being in some cases both an effect of low incomes and, in itself, a reason for poor access to economic opportunities.

In this analysis, many of the problems will evidently not be exclusive to rural areas. Indeed, it can be questioned whether rural deprivation is really rural as peripheral rural areas share with inner urban areas many similar characteristics such as declining demand for labour, low levels of investment, declining public and private services, and housing markets which 'lock in' the poor (Moseley 1980). The work of the Community Development Projects (1977) has indicated the need to look beyond the local area for explanations of these 'problems'. The main difference between the problems of rural and urban areas can either be in the number of people affected by them in specific locations or, more cynically, in the amount of attention (academic and official) focused upon urban areas far outweighing the rural (see, for example, the Community Development Projects 1977; Herbert and Smith 1979).

Economic Opportunities

Rural Incomes Low income households are to be found in rural and urban areas, even if they tend to be more visible in the latter in decaying slums and in high unemployment statistics. In rural areas, both inter-county and intra-county differences exist in income levels. Data sources are unfortunately often unsuitable for an analysis of these due to the coarse spatial classifications adopted; nor are standard regions or counties very useful as they often include substantial urban and rural areas. By county, however, a clear picture emerges of low incomes in peripheral areas of Britain, which has been illustrated by an Inland Revenue Survey of Personal Incomes Statistics. Table 2.1 lists the ten counties with the lowest average incomes in England and Wales and it is evident that the majority of these are peripheral and rural counties. Shucksmith (1981) also illustrates this point, citing research which compares rurality and poverty rankings. Many of the counties from those in Table 2.1 were included: Cornwall, Powys, Gwynedd and Dyfed were the counties with the largest proportions of 'poor' as well as being most rural.

Table 2.1
Ten counties with the lowest average incomes, 1974-1975

County	£
Gwynedd	2,275
Cornwall	2,309
Isle of Wight	2,313
Powys	2,343
Lancashire	2,401
Devon	2,404
Norfolk	2,425
Clwyd	2,453
Durham	2,502
Avon	2,514

Source: after Thomas and Winyard (1979)

These income figures may, of course, be depressed by larger proportions of retired or self-employed in the peripheral areas although, equally, high salary commuters who live in rural villages can inflate average earnings; therefore, these types of data must be used with caution. More convincing, perhaps, are figures that show the earnings by employment categories, as a percentage of national figures. In 1977, male weekly-paid manual workers in the South West and East Anglia were earning only 91.5 per cent and 92.6 per cent, respectively, of the average for Britain as a whole. Similar differences were also to be seen for non-manual workers. The lower rates of pay could be the consequence of a concentration of employment in low pay jobs in, for example, agriculture or services, but equally there could be a distinct rural influence maintaining low wages. Both might be of importance although, if farm workers alone are considered, these emerge as a large and distinctive group amongst the rural low paid. The 1977 New Earnings Survey of the Department of Employment shows that the average weekly pay in agriculture and horticulture was £54.7 compared to the 'all industries' figure of £71.5 (Thomas and Winyard 1979). Well over 40 per cent of agricultural workers could thus be described as low paid (earning less than £50 per week). Against such low pay are often quoted the dubious benefits of cheap or free food and accommodation for agricultural workers. However, it is certainly very debatable whether farmworkers and their families can secure a decent standard of living from such wages and the well-known social problems associated with tied accommodation are discussed later.

Rural areas also tend to have a higher dependency on supplementary benefits and other social security benefits, although this is not universally so. It is suggested that the poverty trap catches a proportionally larger number of rural than of urban workers, in particular agricultural workers' families.

This occurs through the unfavourable operation of direct taxation and welfare state benefits, which makes wage-earners at certain income levels relatively worse off than others earning more or less money but able to claim taxation allowances or social security benefits, respectively. Low levels of trade union partici- pation in many small scale rural industries, farmwork in part- icular, can partially be blamed for the current position (Winyard 1978a; Thomas and Winyard 1979). However, it could also be argued that a certain outlook predisposes rural workers to accept, and remain, in low income employment. This may also tend to reduce the out migration which in turn could reduce *per capita* income inequalities.

Rural employment This theme is obviously very closely associated with the preceding one of rural low pay. Rural employment opportunities are, by the very nature of rural settlement, scat- tered and usually with relatively small scale employers. Many rural residents (excluding the spiralists and urban commuters) are self-employed in services or small manufacturing firms. Relatively few major industrial or service employers are to be found in peripheral locations and, as a result, it may be said that ".... rural employment is characterised by structural imbalance, low economic potential and poor accessibility ...." (Packman 1979, p.51).

Structurally, most rural areas have above the national average employment in agriculture, which is the single most evident characteristic of the labour force. Increased mechanisation and agricultural improvement, referred to earlier in the chapter, have led to a dramatic reduction in the numbers employed in agriculture, by possibly 50 per cent since the 1950s. In June 1976 there were some 140,000 regular full-time workers in agricul- ture in England and Wales, although there was half this number again employed in seasonal work. Labour shedding will probably continue in agriculture and also in agriculturally-related employ- ment such as food processing, transport, and agricultural machinery production, where there is still scope for further mechanisation. This 'indirect' agricultural employment can be of great significance to local economies; Packman (1979) suggests that, in Norfolk, indirect agricultural employment amounts to 6 per cent of the total labour force, compared with 7 per cent in farming jobs.

Manufacturing industry also tends to be under-represented and there are proportionately larger numbers of small scale service employers, large scale service employment tending to locate in major urban centres. However, whilst it is tempting to think of rural employment purely in agriculture/agriculturally- related terms, in many areas, tourism and recreation may provide seasonal employment and also provide seasonal increases in the need for services. This type of work, along with agriculture and professional work, can be shown to be attractive to rural school leavers although, in reality, their chances of obtaining employment outside agriculture and a limited range of services are slim (Gilg 1980a). Some rural areas, notably David Eversley's 'sun-belt' counties of central lowland England, are attractive rural areas and not particularly in need of much assistance. By contrast, the extremely rural areas are those facing the greatest employment problems.

Certain government agencies such as the Council for Small Industries in Rural Areas (CoSIRA) are active in attempting to assist the encouragement of small industrial employers in rural areas although, in the face of stagnation in the national economy, great inroads into the rural employment problem cannot be expected. The generally poor employment prospects naturally reflect upon the young who may migrate from these areas, as has been adequately illustrated in numerous cases (see, for example, Lawton 1973; Gilg 1976). As a result, age structures in some rural areas can become more elderly and, at the same time, little employment may be available for the older unemployed, especially females. The end product is that, particularly when linked with seasonal unemployment, low activity rates and under-employment must be very common in many rural locations.

Access to service provision

Health services In the past, rural areas have frequently been identified as providing more 'healthy' environments than urban areas, although it has also been recognised that rural areas in Britain sometimes have poorer levels of health service provision, even under the National Health Service, the NHS (Howe 1970; Phillips 1981). It is clear that some degree of inadequacy in access to major hospital services will inevitably result from the discrete location of individual facilities amongst spatially continuous, if unevenly distributed, populations (Dear 1974). However, these problems can, in fact, be exacerbated by current trends in health service provision which encourage concentration into health centres and the development of group practices in primary medical services. As a result, Heller (1979) reports a survey of 226 settlements with populations of under 500, of which 87 per cent had no doctor's surgery, 99 per cent, no chemist and 100 per cent, no dentist nor optician. Hence, considerable inadequacy is displayed in rural primary care provision, which is hardly surprising in view of central-isation policies and payments to, for example, general prac-titioners to work in group practices which require large catchment populations. Rural practice allowances are payable but hardly offset the longer distances and travelling involved for some GPs to cover rural areas large enough to include the 2,300 people who are the national average for a GP list.

At one time, it looked very much as if government policy to concentrate hospital provision in Britain would effectively eliminate any true rural hospitals. However, during the 1970s, the Department of Health and Social Security suggested the retention of a number of small hospitals, which might have otherwise faced closure, as community hospitals. The history of this concept goes back to the mid-nineteenth century, to the general practitioner cottage hospital (While 1978), and the policy is a welcome relief from centralisation in health services. It is recognised that the community hospitals will not, of course, provide a full range of diagnostic and treatment facilities but, for certain types of patient such as elderly or chronic sick, they can provide very useful local hospital facilities. Patients, relatives and friends often find the long distances required for visits to centralised facilities to be very trying. These are costs on the community which could well be alleviated by the new policy if fully implemented (Haynes and Bentham 1979). In particular, community hospitals can remove from the large, centralised institutions patients who do not need to be there but, instead, are more in need of temporary in-patient care; this might provide for their eventual 'de-institutionalisation'.

Thus, the personal and social costs of excessive centralisation have been increasingly recognised and there has been a degree of reassessment although, as yet, little retrenchment in the general policy of centralisation of health services. Alternative methods of delivering health care in rural areas have been attempted, such as the provision of part-time clinics in certain locations or the use of mobile units from which to dispense services. The latter have often been disparaged as second best, yet their flexibility in meeting the requirements of scattered or changing populations is unrivalled. Indeed, in some areas, the provision of a variety of health and community services from mobile units seems to be relatively cost-effective (Martin 1976), and this may encourage their use in stringent economic times.

Welfare and social services It has frequently been observed that the NHS and the whole 'paraphernalia' of the welfare state is very much middle-class dominated, with middle-class managers and norms. These social groups include, of course, those who have less frequent recourse to these services, who are more articulate to cope with the bureaucracy involved and who are, in any case, more likely to be personally mobile to attend facilities they need. They are likely to have a telephone to make an appointment and a car in which to keep it, yet, in health services and a range of welfare services, the use rates of social classes one and two are far below those of social classes four and five, which indicates lesser need despite easier physical and social accessibility. It seems that the lower status social groups are least well equipped to deal with the welfare state, either in its social organisation or in accessibility to services. They often have larger families requiring attention and rarely have recourse to private means to help them. Finally, they are more likely to be chronically sick or unemployed and to require a range of assistance from various social service agencies (Blaxter 1976; Brotherston 1976; Cartwright and O'Brien 1976).

In the health services in particular and welfare services in general, there is the notion of the existence of an 'inverse care law', in which those in greatest need of care actually receive the least. This is claimed to act physically in terms of resource provision and socially in terms of access (Hart 1971; Knox 1978; Phillips 1979). If pure expenditure on social services is taken as an indicator (however crude) of provision, then rural counties tend to come off much more poorly than urban county boroughs, as illustrated in Table 2.2.

Table 2.2
Expenditure on selected social services 1973–1974

	Total expen- diture	Res. child- care	Res. elderly – care	Home helps	Day nurs- eries
Rural (Counties)	6,385	2,984	11,075	892	1,219
Urban (C.Boroughs)	9,792	6,888	14,814	1,101	4,026
Percentage shortfall in rural areas	35.0	57.0	26.0	20.0	70.0

All expenditure is measured in £ per 1000 population: res. child- care is per 1000 under 18; res. elderly care and home helps are per 1000 over 65; and day nurseries are per 1000 under 5.

Source: after Stockford (1978)

Even if such figures, based on *per capita* expenditure on selected social services, are only crude indices, there does seem to be a consistent rural shortfall. This can partly be explained by levels of expressed demand in which urban areas have tended to produce the highest levels of demand and political pressure. The folk myth of idyllic rural living conditions is argued as evidence which prevents higher rural resource allocation (Stockford 1978). In this, it is held that extended families support their members, and a clearly defined, understood and respected social structure exists to exclude the need for intrusive, government–promoted levels of social assistance. However, if warnings are true that rural deprivation is, in many ways, as bad as urban deprivation (Moseley 1980), then an inverse care law may well be in operation. It is difficult to say whether the rural ideologies which favour the market, the voluntary and self help rather than public assistance and public provision are responsible. The paternalism of the rural power structure is probably to blame in part. If it is a matter of an imbalance of resource allocation because of 'inner–city infatuation', and a belief that only urban areas have real social problems, then perhaps rural areas should fight this (Larkin 1978a; Cloke and Park 1980).

Education services Few subjects arouse greater intensity of local feeling than the threat of closure of schools, particularly village schools. More than almost anything else, they are seen to give focus and function and to create a community. The main feature of education in rural areas has been reorganisation and consolidation into fewer, larger schools, and primary schools especially have suffered greatly in this process (Martin 1976). There is, of course, considerable debate as to whether children perform better academically in larger or smaller schools in any location but, in rural areas, the major argument against centralisation seems to be that it places a very large burden upon children, especially pre-secondary school age children, to have to travel very far to school every morning and evening.

On economic grounds, it may be claimed that centralisation saves money and also allows a more thorough and extensive syllabus coverage by having a wider range of staff expertise and more demand for individual subjects; this is an argument which receives increased attention in times of restraint in public expenditure. On educational grounds, Watkins (1978) also reports arguments which suggest that small schools may leave much to be desired academically and may even 'disadvantage' pupils, whilst professional isolation can have adverse effects on teaching standards. However, personal attention and lower pupil/teacher ratios may outweigh restrictions in the syllabus and, equally importantly, a village school can provide a physical focus for out-of-hours cultural activities and, as a result, can benefit the larger community.

However, the problem is not merely one of tackling, justifying or preventing school closures in rural areas. There is the practical problem of teaching in remoter locations whilst still achieving academic standards as high as possible, in order to equip local children for very uncertain future job markets, both locally and elsewhere.

Overall, very few researchers have looked specifically at the problems of educational disadvantage in rural settings. General problems such as bad accessibility, poor facilities, difficulties in attracting staff and low levels of resource allocation are discussed (Watkins 1979) and some analysis of differential spending on various educational sectors has been conducted (Taylor and Ayres 1970; Byrne et al 1975) but few explicitly rural works have yet been produced. Data are not easily obtained to examine urban and rural differences, and reliance is often placed on school size as an indicator. The difference between small and large schools, of course, does not necessarily equate solely with rural and urban schools, as there are small schools in urban and suburban areas and quite large country schools also, particularly in the secondary sector. However, the requirement of daily access to schools by children is of great personal importance to families and will be discussed in later chapters.

Access to community and welfare rights information   There is a widely recognised need in modern societies for people to have access to information on a wide variety of economic, social and consumer matters. As Clark and Unwin (1979) point out, much information is available in printed form in libraries, schools, offices and information centres. A great deal of this information is of a basic or even essential nature and its possession certainly contributes to an increasing 'quality of life'. However, isolation (physical and social) is readily identifiable as one of the major features of many rural environments.

To overcome this isolation, a number of strategies can be used to convey a great variety of information to residents in rural areas. Such strategies include mass-media services and specialist ones such as freepost and PRESTEL. Peripatetic mobile information services have also had an important role in the dissemination of information, particularly to rural gatherings at events such as fetes and game fairs. Recreational information is sometimes available at special tourist information centres; and libraries, post offices, doctors' surgeries and other local services can provide display areas for leaflet and poster inform- ation in rural areas. These are very important in 'advertising' the services that are available, because only rarely will a fixed office for many of the facilities be available for personal attendance in small villages. It is essential for reasons of equity and fairness of life opportunities that rural areas are well served by all manner of information outlets. However, even where information is available, it is unfortunately true that it is frequently inadequate or out-of-date; surprisingly, this is true even of the official post office leaflet outlets for Department of Health and Social Security information (Clark and Unwin 1979). Until adequate information guidance is available to all rural residents, an improved knowledge of opportunities and prospects cannot be expected, and their ability to improve their life-chances must inevitably be impaired.

RURAL HOUSING AND SOCIAL JUSTICE

Fundamental to an understanding of all the preceding discussion seems to be the key issue of accessibility, which is directly influenced by where people live. It is a commonplace observation but true that housing is a very important feature in people's lives and, employment apart, it is probably the major influence on their life-styles and chances. Housing provides shelter, a home, and, in its location, allows access to surrounding services and opportunities. The location of a person's residence and his personal mobility will determine broadly his range of social contacts and also how far he can travel to work and to shop, and his children to school. If these distances become too great, then a change of residence becomes necessary or a restriction of activities will result. Local authorities have an important role in regulating access to rural housing, both through direct renting and through controlling new house building. A report by the Department of the Environment (1977, pp.7-8) highlights these roles:

> ".... local authorities, in their dual role of planning authorities and direct providers of housing, should pursue co-ordinated policies which match housing to the prospects for employment and demand. For a wrong decision can be costly: on the one hand, underbuilding may prejudice the economic welfare of rural settlements; on the other, construction for chance sale is dangerous in a small market ...."

Yet, as discussed earlier, Newby et al (1978) have suggested that powerful interests may restrict the building of local authority housing, ostensibly to avoid burdening local ratepayers but also with the 'spin-off' of maintaining some control on workers through the provision of housing tied to their employment. Local power bases may well require examination before a clear picture emerges regarding allocation of resources to various sectors (Rose et al 1979). In addition, local authorities must watch carefully the activities of the private housing market in their rural areas. If, for example, large numbers of commuters and spiralists from urban settlements move in, or too many second homes are purchased, then the prices of local housing may be raised beyond the reach of local residents as illustrated by Shucksmith (1981). Rural workers may become trapped not only in a low wage economy but also in a housing trap from which there is no escape.

It is pertinent to return to the earlier suggestion by Pahl that there is not, in fact, a village population as such. Indeed, in broad (if cynical) terms, three village populations may be discerned: the relatively well-off owner occupiers, largely unconnected with the rural economy as such; the population directly connected with rural employment and living in farms, tied accommodation or other rented or cheap owner-occupied dwellings and, finally, the residents of the local authority estates in villages, whose world is largely unconnected with those of the former. It is with the interlinked problems of these three sectors and, in particular, the management of the local authority sector, that this study is concerned.

The twin themes of social and territorial justice are now familiar to many social scientists and they provide an orientation for this book. The more general of the two is social justice, which implies a certain degree of fairness in society, equity in the allocation of resources rather than pure equality of division. Harvey (1973) was an early proponent of social justice themes, largely in urban settings, and the welfare approach in human geography has researched matters such as the distribution of health, education and social services and less tangible 'welfare rights' matters such as political and social freedom (Smith 1977, 1979).

Territorial justice is a more spatially-based approach which considers the physical distribution of facilities to their user populations. Again, this has largely been developed in urban research (Davies 1968; Pinch 1979). Underlying the whole question of accessibility to services, discussed in the previous section, is the concept that some degree of equity (fairness) should exist in the spatial distribution of resources. Housing, as a key 'service', allows access to other facilities. If access to housing itself is not territorially just, numerous other territorial injustices can follow.

In terms of the broader society, a philosophical question can arise in social and territorial justice as related to housing and rural areas. Should 'non-viable' rural settlements actually be 'kept going' by means of a variety of subsidies for which the whole of society pays? Is it not indeed true that a whole rural settlement pattern may in economic terms be anachronistic and redundant in an age when 'mobility' is ostensibly very easy? It may be argued that this is not the case and that the less well-to-do are the least mobile, have the lowest access to housing resources and often have the least flexibility in employment. This is probably especially true in rural areas but, in research concerned with rural local authority housing, it is not surprising that the topic is approached from a sympathetic stance. Those not supporting this orientation may argue that social justice is best served by the concentration of resources into a few major settlements to maximise economies, whilst 'uneconomic' settlements lose their services and, eventually, fade away. Chapter eight of this book examines matters of social and territorial justice in the allocation of local authority housing and accepts that there is a need to provide this in remoter settlements. Whether such a philosophy can be maintained in the future in the face of financial stringency remains to be seen.

3 Rural housing and the public sector

HOUSING IN RURAL AREAS

The existence of an acute need for improved housing provision in rural areas has been well documented throughout the twentieth century. Fenner Brockway (1932, p.32), commenting upon conditions in East Anglia between the two World Wars, wrote

"I find villages where there is no public sanitary service, where the people themselves empty their earth closets. When they have plots of land they use the excrement for manure, but I find some houses with no gardens and no allotments. It is common to find no water-supply. Sometimes the water has to be carried long distances in pails. Most of the old cottages are unhealthy. The rooms are dark, low and stuffy; the window-space is not much more than a slit in the wall. I find roofs through which the rain drips and walls from which the bricks are falling. There are some good new housing schemes, but it is difficult for an agricultural labourer to pay the rent demanded".

Most commentators would today agree that these stark conditions of overcrowding, poor sanitation and amenities no longer pose such immediate problems. North Oxfordshire provides one of the most striking examples of changes in rural housing, and two surveys of housing conditions by Orwin (1944) and Bates and Cudmore (1975) revealed very substantial improvements in only twenty years. Indeed, the Housing Condition Survey of 1971 suggested that, on balance, rural areas had better levels of household amenities than urban areas (see Rogers 1976, p.89). However, to place this in perspective, it should also be noted that, in the 1976 English House Condition Survey (Department of the Environment 1978), over 5 per cent of the total rural housing stock was still considered to be unfit, and that some of the lowest standards were to be found in such counties as Cornwall, Hereford and Norfolk.

Nevertheless, the real problems of rural housing in the 1980s are widely considered to be those related to the general question of physical, social and economic access. Rural workers, frequently on relatively low wages, find it increasingly difficult to compete in the private housing market. This is partly a result of the pressures on housing supply from the processes of social change, mentioned in chapter two, such as retirement migration, 'rurban-isation', and the growth of second home ownership, and also the planning restrictions on development (Ambrose 1974; Rogers 1976; Larkin 1979).

In order to understand these problems of access to housing, patterns of tenure in rural areas have to be analysed. Table 3.1

compares the tenure distribution in England for rural areas and the country as a whole. This shows that rural areas have smaller proportions of their housing stocks in public ownership and larger proportions in the private sector, whether rented or owner-occupied. However, these differences are not as large as might have been expected and a more sophisticated definition of rural areas would probably have indicated lower proportions of public housing and higher proportions of privately rented dwellings. As will be seen in chapter four, it is evident that some rural areas do have much lower proportions of public housing, sometimes under 20 per cent. It is clear, therefore, that the key to accessibility to rural housing lies within each tenure type. The remainder of this section examines the operation of owner-occupied and privately rented housing while the following sections consider the role of public housing.

Table 3.1
Housing tenure in Great Britain in 1971

Percentages

	Owner-occupied	Privately rented	Local authority rented	Others	Total
Rural areas*	54.5	24.2	21.1	0.2	100.0
England	50.0	21.8	28.0	0.2	100.0

* Defined as the pre-1974 Rural Districts (Dunn et al 1981)

The larger part of the rural housing stock is in the private sector. Throughout both the inter-war and the post-war periods, approximately four-fifths of all new dwellings have been in this sector (Dunn et al 1981), particularly in owner-occupation. The growth of owner-occupancy has partly been encouraged by central government subsidies which, for example, were available for approximately one-fifth of all privately constructed rural houses in the inter-war years. More important have been the influences of income tax allowances (Nevitt 1966) and availability of relatively cheap land in the inter-war decades. This high level of private investment was important in the transformation of the housing conditions noted earlier.

However, these changes have had contrasting implications for the inhabitants of rural areas. New houses have been built in rural areas but their spatial distribution has been uneven; the highest construction rates have been in more urbanised areas, while the lowest rates have occurred in remoter rural areas. This is a reflection of the simple fact that new houses in the rural areas have not really been built for the traditional rural social groups. Instead, the new houses have frequently been built for other 'new' social groups such as the salaried immigrants, spiralists, urban commuters and second home purchasers identified by Pahl and other researchers. The rural working class have fared poorly, in terms of access to owner-occupation, in the face of strong competition from these groups.

In most rural areas, especially those adjacent to urban centres, commuters are the main competitors. The rapid expansion of this group in recent years, which has increased demand and also helped force up house prices, has greatly exacerbated the problems for rural employees (Dunn et al 1981). At the same time, building societies' rules and preferences for mortgage lending favour those in non-manual, secure employment and with higher wages (Boddy 1976), hence tending to exclude many rural workers. Employees in agriculture are especially likely to suffer in this respect (Gasson 1975). The combination of low rural wages, poor mortgage potential and escalating prices are therefore likely to pose substantial barriers to entry into this sector, as the work of Dunn et al (1981) has shown.

The demand for second homes has also added to these difficulties in some areas. Second home ownership in England and Wales has increased rapidly since the mid-1950s (Vane 1975) and numbers are estimated to have increased from around 25,000 in 1945 to 200,000 in 1970 (Rogers 1976). Although not all second homes are owner-occupied, the vast majority are, and the proportion which is rented is estimated to be only between 5 per cent (Vane 1975) and 15 per cent (Bollom 1978) in particular areas although, as costs rise, increasing numbers of second home owners rent out these homes for part of the year. Their regional distribution shows a preponderance in Wales, East Anglia, the South East, the South West and the Lake District, reflecting both the accessibility and the leisure and scenic attractions of such areas, a theme returned to in chapters four and five.

In some locations, second homes can form considerable proportions of the housing stock: for example, 14 per cent of the housing stocks in Anglesey and Merioneth are estimated to be second homes, and in some parishes this rate exceeds 50 per cent (Bollom 1978). As no more than about 50 per cent of second homes were specially built for this purpose (Dower 1977), second home purchasers are often competing directly with local inhabitants in rural areas; this is corroborated by Vane's (1975) study in North Wales which showed that 45 per cent of second homes had been bought from local owners. Shucksmith (1981, p.49) also demonstrates that, in the Lake District, only 48 per cent of house purchasers were local, with more than half the purchases being for holiday accommodation, second homes, or for retirement. As second home owners tend to be in higher paid professional and managerial jobs and are able to buy properties outright with cash, rural workers find it difficult to compete (Bielckus et al 1972). Their actual impact on the local housing market may be even greater given the selectiveness of second home purchasers who tend to buy larger and older, detached houses (Bielckus et al 1972). Although there is no conclusive evidence of the link between house prices and second home ownership (Vane 1975), it is difficult to believe that this can have any effects other than adverse ones for the 'primary' rural population.

While increased competition has affected the demand for rural housing, the supply side has also changed in recent years. Surprisingly little is known about the structure of the construction industry, especially in rural areas (a notable exception is a Department of the Environment report of 1981). However, it seems that the increasing dominance of the building industry by larger, national companies has led to development being concentrated in larger estates, invariably in the larger villages (Rogers 1976). This trend has been reinforced by the key settlement policies (and linked attitudes to planning applications) of many local authorities, so that smaller villages and hamlets tend to have had lower construction rates. There has also been a tendency for larger and more expensive houses to be constructed (Jacobs 1974), so that the provision of new housing has not tended to favour groups of lower income rural inhabitants. In summary then, the interaction of supply and demand has led to highly inequitable access to the owner-occupied sector, especially for those employed in rural areas.

Access to a good standard of privately rented dwellings may also be difficult. This sector has been in decline nationally throughout the twentieth century and, in rural areas, this has been particularly acute since 1974, when the Rent Act gave increased security of tenure to tenants. Leaving aside, for now, tied accommodation, according to Larkin (1979, p.74), the result has been that ".... there are virtually no permanent regulated lettings in rural areas. The only lettings that are often available are by wealthy owner-occupiers who may, for example, spend a year abroad and let their house out at a rent beyond the reach of the lower income families".

In some areas, especially in coastal regions, there may be winter lets available. These provide accessible but only temporary expedients for the rural poor, often leading to the need for transfer to very inadequate housing or, possibly, a caravan during the summer. It is mobile homes or caravans rather than winter lets which most frequently serve to meet the demand for non-tied privately rented accommodation in rural areas. They can form a substantial proportion of all accommodation in an area and, although they may be of variable price and quality, more often than not they act as ".... the true ghettos of the rural poor ...." (Larkin 1979, p.75). Residents of such accommodation may realistically be termed 'trapped', as they are unable to enter owner-occupation and as there are few alternative privately rented dwellings available. Their only alternative would seem to lie in the public sector, although signs here are far from hopeful as there is evidence that rural housing authorities themselves may use caravans as the dumping ground for their homeless families (Shelter 1970).

The stress of being housed in tied accommodation, although different, may be no less acute. Agricultural cottages are not the only type of tied rural accommodation (the Forestry Commission and the Ministry of Defence also have substantial holdings) but they are the most numerous, estimated as being between 70,000 and 80,000 in England and Wales (Gasson 1975) with

31

a further 20,000 in Scotland (Irving and Hilgendorf 1975).

Although the absolute number has declined by a third in England and Wales since 1947, the shrinkage of the agricultural labour force has been even greater, so that, in proportionate terms, the provision of tied accommodation has increased. Thus, the percentage of full-time hired male agricultural workers living in tied accommodation rose from 35 per cent in 1947 to 54 per cent in 1972 (Gasson 1975). As with second homes, there are distinctive regional variations in the provision of this type of accommodation. The highest levels of provision are in Yorkshire, Lancashire and Wales, while Somerset, Devon and Cornwall (which have an average level of provision of 53.9 per cent) have experienced the most rapid post-war decline in tied accommodation. At the intra-regional scale, Gasson (1975) has also shown that tied accommodation is more likely to occur either in very remote areas (where there are few alternatives) or near to towns (where competition for housing is greatest).

There are three aspects of housing need associated with tied accommodation. The first relates to the condition of these dwellings: Irving and Hilgendorf (1975) have shown that farmworkers living in tied accommodation are more likely than those in non-tied accommodation to live in older and smaller dwellings. They are also more likely to be poorly located relative to services; for example, only 48 per cent of tied compared to 71 per cent of non-tied accommodation was located within a mile of the nearest shop, and similar differences also existed for primary and secondary schools. Fletcher (1969), in a study of housing conditions in Tiverton in Devon, also found that the standard of amenities in agricultural tied cottages was far worse than in owner-occupied and local authority housing but better than in the remainder of the privately rented sector.

The second aspect of tied cottages is that it is the lowest paid agricultural employees who are most likely not to be accommodated in these (Gasson 1975), and hence those probably in the greatest need may even have even worse private provision. In each of the cases outlined above - either of the agricultural worker not provided with tied accommodation, or provided with an unsatisfactory dwelling - the alternatives available are limited, and most are likely to have to turn to the local authority sector rather than to any other type of tenure (Gasson 1975).

The third aspect of need related to tied cottages is the most publicised one, namely the constant problem of eviction. In the early 1970s there were estimated to be about 1,000 - 1,500 evictions every year and they occurred most frequently in the region with the fewest accommodation alternatives available, that is in South East England (Gasson 1975; Rogers 1976). As the term implies, tied accommodation is linked to employment, so a worker who loses his job, resigns or retires may also lose his home. More recently there has been greater legal protection for these tenants. The Agricultural Act 1970 allowed for eviction to be deferred for at least six months although farmers could avoid this restriction if they could show that they needed a particular cottage for the efficient operation of their farm. Later, the Rent (Agriculture) Act 1976 extended the same security of tenure to tied accommodation that existed for the remainder of the privately rented sector (Clements 1978). This also covered the position of wives and husbands after the deaths of their spouses and after retirement. Farmers could only reclaim such cottages if they could demonstrate they were required for other key employees, in which case the rehousing of the evicted families became a priority consideration for the local authority housing department.

As introduced in chapter two, the provision of tied accommodation can be identified as one reason for low rates of local authority housing involvement in rural areas. Farmers, as important local ratepayers, may wish to keep building to a minimum to keep rates down. Instead, farm workers would be housed in tied accommodation, with other additional benefits ".... not the least of which were the convenience of having workers on call, the greater stability tied housing conferred on the labour force, and the reinforcement of ties of dependency ...." (Newby 1979, p.184). So, as Newby remarks, whether as ratepayers or as employers, farmers who run the majority of rural councils may find it advantageous to provide tied housing for their workers and to build the minimum number of local authority houses.

This brief review of the private rented and owner-occupied sectors has indicated that considerable problems of access existed in both tenures for less prosperous rural inhabitants. Even agricultural workers who 'benefit' from tied accommodation can find this to be a source of acute housing stress. For them, and for many other poorer rural residents (whether retired or employed in rural industries or services), the local authority sector can often provide the only alternative to their existing dwellings and their main hope of improved accommodation. The role that the local authority does play will be considered in the following section.

THE DEVELOPMENT OF PUBLIC HOUSING

The history of public housing in Britain is discussed in a number of text books and need only be reviewed briefly here (Berry 1974; Lansley 1979). Individual local authorities built public housing for rent from the 1860s, but these were mainly in larger cities such as Glasgow and Liverpool in response to the health hazards and political difficulties posed by urban slums (Gauldie 1974). The first national act enabling local authorities to build housing for direct renting was the 1890 Public Health Act, but this was very restrictive and largely ineffective. Therefore, the Addison Act 1919 is usually considered to be the real starting point of the public sector housing programme. This laid upon local authorities the obligation of building new houses to meet the needs in their areas. It provided generous financial subsidies and, although these were subsequently reduced (Orbach 1977), some 170,000 new local authority houses were built under the provisions of this Act. The Act, however, made no specific provisions for rural areas even though the Salisbury Panel had previously recommended that 50,000 houses had to be built just to meet their need alone (Orbach 1977). Perhaps this omission is not so surprising in the light of the argument that the Act was passed very much in response to the Glasgow rent strikes of 1915 and pre-war industrial unrest, both of which were mainly urban features (Community Development Project 1976).

The Chamberlain Housing Act of 1923, which changed the basis of housing subsidies to a less generous flat rate, likewise made no special provision for rural areas. Only with the 1924 Housing Act (the Wheatley Act) did such provision emerge. This Act, while continuing with flat rate subsidies per house, differentiated between urban areas (£9) and rural areas (£12-10-0d) in recognition of their differential costs. When the flat rate subsidies were later decreased in 1927, this differential was retained, £11 being payable per house in rural areas compared with £7-10-0d in urban areas (Berry 1974, p.39).

These early acts had aimed at provision to meet general housing needs but the emphasis was shifted by the Greenwood Act 1930, which switched attention to slum clearance rehousing (the earlier acts were operative only until 1933). However, this did retain the urban-rural differential; a subsidy of £2-10-0d was payable in agricultural parishes compared to £2-5-0d in urban parishes. Furthermore, an additional £1 per person was payable when agricultural workers were rehoused. The 1935 Housing Act which soon followed for the relief of overcrowding, had a similar aim to the Greenwood Act and maintained the higher rural subsidy.

Although the various housing acts since 1924 had made special provisions for rural areas, they seem to have been less successful than had been hoped. Only about 20 per cent of rural construction was in the public sector in this period (Dunn et al 1981). Perhaps a major reason for this was that the most active authorities in house building in the inter-war period were those which were controlled by the Labour Party, and these were predominantly in urban areas (Community Development Project 1976). Weak local finances and a serious doubt as to the ability of farmworkers to pay local authority rents may also have deterred the building of rural council housing.

Post-war housing policy under the Labour government saw a return to the ideal of public housing to meet general needs and a major shift from private to public housing. At the same time, a differential subsidy was maintained, £25-10-0d being paid in agricultural areas compared to £16-10-0d in other districts. Subsidies were also allowed from the local rates, up to £1-10-0d in agricultural areas and £5-10-0d in all other areas. When the Conservative government came to power in 1951, it set out to change the public/private balance in house building. At first, however, in recognition of the condition of the building industry, the emphasis was on public housing, with subsidies being increased for both agricultural areas (to £35–14–0d) and other areas (to £26–14–0d). Gradually a change in emphasis did occur. Subsidy levels were reduced in 1954 and slum clearance objectives replaced provision for general needs.

Thereafter, a degree of consensus existed in the 1960s between Labour and Conservative governments. Both favoured the switch from renewal to improvement policies, as advocated in the 1964 and 1969 Housing Acts. Both also seemed committed to an even balance in provision between public and private construction. This consensus was effectively ended with the return of a Conservative government in 1970 which favoured the private sector and encouraged the sale of council houses; as a result, approximately 100,000 were sold between 1970 and 1974. The most controversial aspect of housing policy during this period, however, was the 1972 Housing Finance Act, which sought to simplify and unify housing subsidies within the public sector and between it and the private sector. There was also a provision for 'fair rents' for council houses to be determined centrally and it was this proposal (which effectively raised rents in many areas) that led to the Act being opposed by several Labour controlled councils, the best known case being that of Clay Cross (Berry 1974).

This legislation was quickly repealed by the succeeding Labour government in 1975. Labour had also promised a thorough review of housing policy as a whole. However, its Housing Policy Review of 1977 essentially favoured the 'status quo'. Nevertheless, Labour did introduce the Housing Investment Programmes in 1977 which recognised the wider roles that local authority housing departments had adopted in many areas. Under these provisions, the housing authorities were to assess total housing need in their areas, and more flexible subsidies were made available to cover expenditure under three headings: first, expenditure on public sector house building, acquisition and renovation; secondly, improvement grants and mortgages for the private sector; and thirdly, lending to housing associations (Watson et al 1979).

The next major landmark in housing policy was the Housing Act 1980 which, according to Schifferes (1980a, p.10), introduced the ".... most far reaching changes in the council housing system since its effective origins at the end of the First World War". This wide ranging Bill made three main proposals for the local authority sector. These were the provision of a tenant's charter (which tended to reduce security of tenure for 'other' relatives), a new subsidy system (which tended to act as a disincentive for new building by councils), and the 'Right-to–buy' for tenants. Local authorities have been permitted to sell houses for more than forty years and, indeed, some 260,000 council and new town houses have been sold since 1951 (Watson 1980). This Bill is different, however, in that it gives all tenants of more than three years' standing the statutory right to buy. The price is fixed as that which the house would realise if sold on the open market, subject to a discount of 33 per cent for the first four years and 1 per cent for each complete year thereafter, up to a maximum of 50 per cent. Under favourable market conditions it has been estimated that sales could rise to 125-175,000 a year (Building Trades Journal 1980). Many commentators have expressed concern that this will eventually lead to authorities being left with a residue of the least desirable and most expensive to manage dwellings.

This may well cause particular problems in rural areas, especially if properties are resold as second homes. Some of these special concerns are recognised in the Bill, which has placed restrictions on resales in Areas of Outstanding Natural Beauty, National Parks and areas designated by the Secretary of State as 'rural areas'; in these areas, either houses can only be resold to someone who has lived or worked in the area for three years immediately preceding, or, during the first ten years, the Council must be allowed first refusal on resale. This is clearly an attempt to retard the resale of council houses to outsiders moving into attractive rural areas. Even so, in these and in other rural areas, sales are bound to affect the opportunities for those on waiting or transfer lists (see Gilg 1981). The proposed reductions in government expenditure on housing, which were outlined in the 1980 White Paper on public expenditure (Aughton 1980), are further likely to increase these difficulties.

In summary, two features of the development of public housing should be noted. First, almost since the inception of local authority involvement in housing, there have been special financial provisions to stimulate building in rural areas. Nevertheless, they have not been as successful as might have been anticipated and consequently this tenure is relatively less important in rural than in urban areas. This may be especially significant given recent policy initiatives in the realm of council house sales. Secondly, the various housing acts with their different objectives and subsidies have led to a considerable variety of house types being constructed. Donnison (1979, p.131) stated, with respect to inner cities, that ".... council housing used to be a pretty standard product. Now it may be anything from a well-equipped modern house on a plum site overlooking the park or the river to a grotty flat in a dreary and distant estate or a slum acquired for long-postponed demolition ....". These remarks can be seen to apply equally well to rural areas. Local authorities possess a variety of council houses and are faced with the housing needs of a variety of social groups. Although the roles of the housing authorities have been broadened in recent years, rented local authority houses remain their primary resource. Therefore, it is their major responsibility to try to match housing needs with their available housing stock. The managerial approaches which have been adopted to further this responsibility are reviewed in the following section.

MANAGING LOCAL AUTHORITY HOUSING

In recent years there has been considerable research on the operation of local housing authorities, inspired by the analytical approach already referred to, known as urban managerialism. This approach is best exemplified by the work of Pahl (1970), who considered that there were managers of the urban system who acted as 'gatekeepers', controlling access to resources and facilities. Research has therefore focused on the managers of local authority housing departments (and to a much lesser extent on the local councillors) who control the allocation of council housing.

In his original formulation of this approach, Pahl (1970, p.215) emphasised that these managers exerted ".... an independent influence on the allocation of scarce resources ....". More recently, Pahl (1975) has sought to pay less attention to the autonomy of the managers and rather to emphasise their role within the broader social formation (see Duncan 1977). Others have questioned the role of 'independent arbiter' assigned to the managers (Lambert et al 1978) and emphasise the wider economic influences on the demand and supply of council housing, its ideological role (Gray 1976b) and its relationship to the value of labour power (Ball 1978). The authors of this book share this concern for reorienting the study of housing, but also consider that the study of the operations of the local housing authorities is important. The thesis of 'managerialism' may be rejected but the practices of the managers are still of interest, especially in rural areas where there have been very few studies of housing management. At this point, therefore, the focus is still on the intermediate level of allocation for consumption, rather than at the higher level of production, capital accumulation and state policies.

The importance of broadening the range of case studies of housing management lies in the scope for variation in local practices. There is no clear definition of what should constitute the function of a local authority housing department (Cullingworth 1979). It is true that housing authorities have certain statutory obligations to fulfil. These include rehousing from slum clearance schemes, emergency provision for the homeless and, in rural areas under the Rent (Agriculture) Act 1976, rehousing families from tied accommodation. Even in these three circumstances, there is scope for varied interpretation of the provision required. Some individuals may not be rehoused from slum clearance schemes, particularly lodgers and those who are considered to have moved into the area after compulsory purchase orders have been served (Gray 1976a). The homeless are often treated differently in terms of rehousing according to whether they are considered to be avoidably or unavoidably without homes (Lambert et al 1978), while, in the case of agricultural workers in tied cottages, there is some ambiguity over the interpretation by housing authorities of the reasons for the termination of their present employment (Schifferes 1980c).

Even greater variation exists in the management of housing

outside these statutory obligations. This is particularly so in the two main sources of expressed need for local authority housing; these are the waiting list and the transfer list. The remainder of this section examines how these are managed and the various allocation policies adopted by housing departments.

Waiting lists represent the major source of expressed housing need in that individual families must actually apply to be placed on such a list and they also have to provide details of their present domestic circumstances. Even so, such lists do not represent all housing needs. There is evidence that many people living in very poor conditions will only approach the housing department when an actual crisis arises (Lambert et al 1978), and many authorities operate restrictions on entry onto their waiting lists. Recent surveys by Macey (1980) and Winyard (1978b) have indicated that only some 13 to 17 per cent of English authorities have completely open waiting lists with no restrictions. Most are restricted to those who are already resident in, or are employed in, the local authority area. Even residence may not be a sufficient criterion for inclusion, as about one-quarter of local authorities operate a residential qualifying period (Macey 1980). For example, in Birmingham in the early 1970s, new arrivals could only be placed on the 'register of enquiries' during the first five years and, even after their transfer to the general section of the housing register, there was a further six-month delay before they could be con- sidered for rehousing (Lambert et al 1978). Length of residence is not the only criterion used and some authorities exclude individuals from the waiting list on the basis of their age or of being owner occupiers (Niner 1975). Although there have been a succession of appeals to make all waiting lists truly open (Cullingworth 1979), there is no clear evidence that sub- stantial progress has been made in this direction (Macey 1980). Furthermore, with reference to the exclusion of large numbers of people from waiting lists by means of residential qualifications and rules which prevent certain categories from applying, it has been suggested that " .... such restrictions tend to be more common and draconian in rural than in urban areas ...." (Larkin 1979, p.72).

A place on the waiting list is, of course, no guarantee of being rehoused, because those on the waiting list are ranked, usually by one of three methods. First, some authorities (about one-quarter according to Winyard 1978b) operate simple queues on a 'first come, first served' basis. Unless there are very short waiting lists, this method will be insensitive to actual housing need (Cullingworth 1979). Secondly, a few authorities operate 'merit schemes', under which each applicant is evaluated by a committee. This is really an informal version of the third method, the points scheme, which is used in most areas.

Points schemes allocate scores to applicants on the basis of a number of criteria. These are variable but usually incor- porate the length of time on the waiting list, overcrowding, sanitation, sharing, medical needs, family size and housing amenities (Berry 1974; Niner 1975). It is this, the points system, which effectively identifies those who are likely to be rehoused. In Hull, Gray (1976a) considered that the points scheme and other rules effectively reduced the 16,000 on the waiting list to approximately one-third of this number who could actually be considered to be in need. In practice, the points schemes are considered to favour married couples, larger families, those born locally and those living in insanitary, shared and/or overcrowded dwellings. However, there is no real uniformity in these schemes, so that applicants might be ranked very differently according to the authority to which they have applied. Furthermore, although it has long been argued that the criteria used in points schemes should be publicised (Cullingworth 1979), it is estimated that about one-fifth of all housing authorities treat them as being strictly confidential (Macey 1980). Many applicants may therefore have no clear notion of the criteria according to which they have been assessed by their housing department, and may naturally feel aggrieved when their subjectively-felt reasons for requiring housing are apparently ignored or discounted.

After they have been 'pointed', applicants are then placed in queues for different types of accommodation. These are usually differentiated by the size of the house needed, but other criteria such as the type of dwelling (flat, house, bungalow) and pre-ferred area may also be used. These queues have different average waiting times and Gray (1976a) in Hull, not surprisingly, found that the shortest wait was likely to occur in the queue for flats. Therefore, for any applicant, the probability of being rehoused depends on a number of factors, including the 'openness' of the waiting list, the type of points scheme used, and the queues formed for different types of accommodation; and all of these are likely to vary amongst authorities.

The other major source of expressed housing need is the transfer/exchange list operated by most authorities. This includes local authority tenants who wish to exchange their existing accommodation or to be transferred into a vacant tenancy. Adjustment of house size to take into account changes in family size, improved accessibility to services or employment, proximity to relatives, or a preference for an alternative type of dwelling (usually a house with a garden), are frequently given as the reasons for these transfer/exchange requests. Usually the only restriction placed on acceptance onto the transfer list is that no previous move has been made during a specified period in the immediate past.

When it comes to the actual allocation of dwellings, the housing department is faced with two major managerial decisions. The first relates to the priority to be assigned to the rehousing of different groups of applicants. Niner (1975) has shown that priority is usually given to rehousing from clearance areas (and now also to the homeless) as there is a statutory obligation for this. The next priority is given either to applicants with medical grounds for rehousing or to those on the transfer list; the latter may be encouraged especially if it involves elderly persons who wish to vacate larger houses for which they now no longer feel the need (thus releasing such houses for other tenants). The lowest priority is usually accorded to those on the general needs waiting list. These priorities are reflected in the average waiting times for rehousing; in Hull, these were 2 to 3 months in clearance areas, 7 months for those on transfer lists, and 10 years for those on waiting lists (Gray 1976a).

The second managerial decision for the housing department is the allocation of particular applicants to specific dwellings. Most authorities grade both tenants and accommodation. Tenants are usually graded by housing visitors, frequently in terms of their rent-paying and house-keeping abilities. The Central Housing Advisory Committee (1969, para.96) found that "Moral rectitude, social conformity, clean living and a 'clean' rent book on occasion seemed to be essential qualifications for eligibility ....". Invariably, these gradings are likely to differ amongst housing authorities. Popplestone (1979, p.35), in a study of six authorities, wrote that ".... noisy parties, unkempt gardens, too many pets and rent arrears may be tolerated in some areas and by some people but cause annoyance in others ... Difficult families from one estate ... would have been regarded by families in another district ... as nothing out of the ordinary". The housing stock is also graded and this is mainly by its age (Gray 1976a); Lambert et al 1978), although physical condition may also be assessed directly. This has become increasingly important, given the increased variation which exists in the types of council houses available.

After properties and applicants have been graded, housing management then tries to match the two. Frequently, this has already been done when grading the tenants. For example, Gray (1976a) found that, in Hull, the housing visitors made recommendations such as 'Fair only – suitable for pre-war property' or 'Excellent tenant – suitable for new property'. In these cases, allocation is then simply a matter of waiting for a suitably graded dwelling to become vacant for the priority applicant to be rehoused. Applicants can, of course, refuse the accommodation offered, but this is very difficult. Those in immediate housing crisis have no real option but to accept their first offer. Even those with less immediate stress may be reluctant to refuse the accommodation offered; there is no guarantee that the next offer will be any better and, after two or three refusals, an applicant may be downgraded within the waiting or transfer list.

A number of consequences is likely to follow from the procedures outlined. One is that, given the limited 'choice' of housing available to, and/or offered to, most applicants, a high degree of frustrated mobility is likely to exist among tenants (Bird 1976). Furthermore, as houses of similar types are likely to be spatially clustered, these allocation methods are likely to contribute to social segregation (Gray 1976a), and this may actively be encouraged by some authorities so as ".... to maximize harmony between neighbours with similar life styles ...." (Burns 1979). The most publicised feature of these methods is the formation of 'sink' estates for what are termed 'problem families', an objective frequently justified as it minimises management problems (Burns 1979). There are a number of studies of such estates and the restricted life chances and stigmatisation which are associated with them (for example, see Weightman 1978). Taylor (1979) reminds us that they are 'difficult-to-let, difficult-to-live-in and sometimes difficult-to-get-out-of', unless the tenants have the necessary medical reports.

This brief review has indicated that considerable variation exists in housing management policies and in their social consequences for people living in, hoping to move in to, or to exchange council houses. It is significant that most of the research which has been reviewed so far concerns urban areas, especially for the conurbations. The final section of this chapter examines the particular features of rural local authority housing which are to be discussed in the remainder of this book.

Local authority housing in rural areas

In contrast to the relative wealth of studies on local authority housing and its management in urban areas, relatively little is known about these rural areas. Niner (1975) has published a comparative study of six local authorities, one of which, Ludlow, is predominantly rural. The analyses of residential qualifications and point systems revealed no real differences between urban and rural areas, although slightly more attention is given in the latter to location as a criterion of 'unsuitable accommodation'. That the practices of the housing managers should be broadly similar in urban and rural areas is hardly surprising, in view of their unified training. However, although the management methods are alike, the problems they are applied to, and their consequences, are different since (as argued in chapter two) rural areas tend to experience certain problems not really evident in urban settings.

Two features in particular are important: the overall provision of housing, and its location, and these are clearly linked. The question of overall provision has already been touched upon. The growth of local authority housing in rural areas has tended to lag behind national trends, even though special provision for higher subsidies has been included in some of the Housing Acts (Rogers 1976). Rural authorities therefore tend to have smaller proportions of their housing stock in public ownership, and this is compounded by the limited housing association activity in these rural areas (Institute of Housing 1979). Although the overall local authority provision is lower, need is not necessarily lower. Indeed, in addition to the 'normal' housing need, rural areas may be faced with particular needs such as those of agricultural workers being evicted from tied cottages (Jones 1975). There may also be other pressures; for example, Vane (1975) has indicated that in at least one county in North Wales the number of retirement and second homes exceeded the number of council houses. The implication is clear, that waiting lists and transfer lists are likely to be just as long in rural as in urban areas. Indeed, Larkin (1979) has shown that frequently they may be longer; in his survey, he found that some 6 to 8 per cent of all households were on the waiting lists in the larger metropolitan areas such as Birmingham and Manchester, compared with rates of 9 to 14 per cent in rural areas such as Derwentside and New Forest. A study of West Oxfordshire (see Larkin 1979) also indicated that applicants in villages usually had to wait longer to be rehoused than those in towns.

Overall provision is also related to the second feature, location. Compared with urban authorities, rural housing authorities generally have smaller stocks, spread over geographically larger areas with relatively diffuse populations. The locations of council houses may therefore be unevenly matched with the existing settlement pattern (Larkin 1978b). This is very much reinforced by the tendency for houses to be built in a few centres, rather than to be widely distributed; reasons for this include the key settlement approach of planning policies, the economies of scale of construction and infrastructure provision (Rogers 1976), the higher costs of using matching local materials in some villages (Larkin 1979), and lower management and repair costs. Larkin considers that the reform of local government in 1974, which grouped urban and rural districts together, has further strengthened this trend. This is borne out by the West Oxfordshire study which showed that 67 per cent of new council houses were built in the main towns which had only 42 per cent of all the applicants.

In consequence, applicants in rural areas are likely to have a reduced choice of accommodation and may find it more difficult to be rehoused locally or in proximity to employment/service opportunities. The West Oxfordshire study again provides evidence for this: only 52 per cent of applicants in villages compared to 71 per cent in the towns were rehoused in the same settlement. Those living in the rural areas were therefore likely to be rehoused at a greater distance from their present home. Another extreme example is provided by those living in agricultural tied cottages; Irving and Hilgendorf (1975) have shown that almost one-third of all tied cottages are at least two miles distant from the nearest council house, let alone a vacant one. Newby et al (1978) have highlighted how easily farmers have obtained planning permission to build new accommodation for workers on their farms, whereas the problems of accessibility are more likely to be alleviated by a more even spread of local authority housing. Conversely, the massive council house sales which are now underway can only exacerbate the problems of access to local authority houses in rural Britain by reducing already small stocks.

SECTION B

A CASE STUDY OF RURAL HOUSING IN SOUTH DEVON

4 A rural district in a rural county

One of the main contentions of this book is that local authority housing, by virtue of its importance to lower income groups, assumes an equal, if not greater significance, in a rural locality than that which it occupies in an urban area. The nature, location and availability of local authority housing are crucial to the lives of residents depending upon it and, to date, only very general statements or urban examples have been produced specifically on these themes. The research now discussed focuses on one important rural district in the county of Devon and it is the aim of this chapter to set the context for the following empirical chapters. This current chapter falls into two main sections. The first discusses the county of Devon as a whole, particularly the characteristics which make it suitable as a setting for a case study of local authority involvement in rural housing, its settlement patterns and its housing policies. The second section of the chapter then introduces more specific aspects of the case study area, the South Hams, a district located in the south of the county. The scene is then set for the first of the empirical chapters, chapter five, which looks in detail at the housing stock of the South Hams and the particular role of local authority housing in it.

DEVON: A RURAL COUNTY

The geographical county of Devon is the third largest in England, whilst the population in 1981 was barely 950,000 persons. These facts alone mean that population densities will be relatively sparse in British terms. When it is considered that over one-half of these people live in the three urban concentrations of Plymouth (1981 population 243,900), Exeter (1981 population 95,600) ,and Torbay (1981 population 115,600), it will be evident that considerable polarisation of densities occurs.

The nature of this polarisation has been influenced by recent population changes. Broadly speaking, the county has received a net inflow of migrants in recent years. Between 1951 and 1961, the population increased by some 26,100, 18,800 of which was due to in-migration. Between 1961 and 1971 population grew more markedly by 75,700, of which 64,800 was due to net migration. This has been a very interesting trend and, by the mid-1970s, natural increase had actually altered to a natural decrease, offset by continued in-migration in older age groups. This is a second important demographic trend in Devon, the increasing proportion of older persons due to in-migration around the age of retirement. As a result, the proportion of people over 65 years of age has increased from 140 per thousand in 1951 to 187 per thousand in 1971. This compares with figures of 111 per thousand (1951) and 134 per thousand (1971) for

England and Wales as a whole. In addition, the proportion of people in the younger, economically active age group 15-44 was falling during this period (even if absolute numbers showed an increase).

The distribution of population in Devon is of course of considerable interest as background to the present study. Cloke (1979) notes three constituent parts to the pattern. First, certain parishes fall within the spheres of influence of major settlements, such as Exeter, Plymouth, Torbay and Barnstaple (locations may be seen in Figure 4.1), and thus they tend to be relatively densely populated. This has taken the form of a suburban collar around Plymouth with sectoral growth interspersed with smaller settlements around some of the other urban foci such as Exeter.

Secondly, certain coastal and a few inland parishes have benefited from the impact of tourism and retirement migration, typically on the south east Devon coastline (settlements such as Sidmouth, Exmouth, Budleigh, Seaton and Dawlish/Teignmouth are examples). Finally, the largest area of the county is covered by substantial numbers of small settlements, occasionally interrupted by larger villages or market towns. In particular, the north, north-west, west and centre of Devon fall into this category, along with some remoter areas in the far south of Devon in the South Hams, the district with which this book is concerned. "These parts of Devon form an excellent example of an anachronistic settlement pattern which was originally geared to agricultural production but which is outmoded under present economic regimes ...." (Cloke 1979, p.166-167).

From this tripartite division it is clear that population growth has been concentrated in four main areas: the Barnstaple/Braunton area; parishes immediately surrounding Torbay; some coastal parishes in the south and east; and an outer ring of parishes surrounding Exeter and Plymouth. Some parishes within the South Hams District of South Devon can be identified among the last three growth areas, although the South Hams also has within it areas of sparse population, particularly in the north along the edges of Dartmoor.

The general picture of a rural county can be supplemented by reference to an 'index of rurality' (Cloke 1977). Plymouth and environs apart, none of Devon is identified as being under 'pressure', and much of the county falls into Cloke's categorisation of 'extreme rural' or 'intermediate rural'. This particularly applies to the north-west, west and central areas of the county. Devon is, in many ways, pervaded by a sense of rurality which belies the population even of the most urbanised areas. Perhaps this accounts for its popularity as a destination for tourism, retirement and second homes. Rurality is certainly reflected in the employment and economic bases of the county which are considered next.

Economic changes are closely linked with the demographic trends outlined. The sectoral distribution of employment in Devon, compared with the rest of the South West Region and

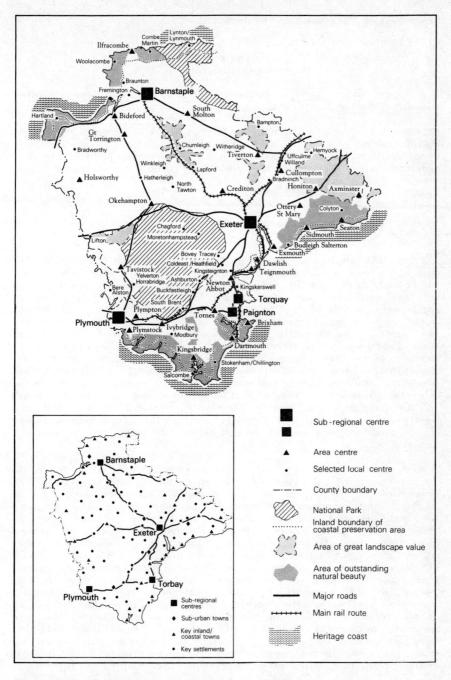

Figure 4.1: Settlement pattern in Devon 1979
(Inset: settlement pattern in the early 1970s)
Sources: after Devon County Council (1972, 1979)

Great Britain, is shown in Table 4.1.

Table 4.1
Employment structure in 1974

| Industrial Sector | Devon | | S.W. Region | Great Britain |
	Total	%	%	%
Primary	16,500	5	4	3
Manufacturing	75,300	23	30	35
Construction	25,800	8	6	6
Services	209,400	64	60	56
Total	327,000	100	100	100

Source: Devon County Council (1977)

From this table, a somewhat larger proportion than nationally
may be seen in primary industries (predominantly agriculture
in Devon) and also in service industries. Although traditionally
service industries are considered to give greater stability of
employment to regions, it must be pointed out that, in Devon,
much service employment is, in fact, seasonal and relatively
low paid. Traditionally in Devon, unemployment has fallen
from February and March through to July (when new school
leavers enter the job market) due to the influence of tourist,
agricultural and building activities picking up from spring
onwards. Manufacturing industry is generally lacking in Devon
and two areas of closely monitored land-use are to be found
in the county, one wholly (Dartmoor National Park) and one
partly (Exmoor National Park). Industrial development, even
if it was desired, would be curtailed in these two substantial
areas.

Average earnings in all income ranges are also lower in
Devon than in the rest of the South West and England. The
proportion of employees in low earning categories tends to be
higher, and average differentials between Devon and England
for male manual workers were a little over £9 per week in
1976 (Devon County Council 1977). However, it should be pointed
out that such figures can be misleading in aggregate terms
as returns on full-time weekly earnings do not take account
of important monies which accrue to many residents of the county
from sources such as pensions and investments. Nevertheless,
people in the economically active categories who are not paid
according to nationally agreed rates do appear to suffer. In
social terms this can be very serious as the South West, in
general, and parts of Devon in particular, have been becoming
very expensive as places in which to live, as illustrated by
home purchase prices which tend to be relatively high in this
region compared with other parts of the country (Table 4.2).

Table 4.2
Regional variations in average house prices, 1979

Region	Average Price (£)
Greater London	25,793
South West	20,494
East Anglia	18,461
South East	24,675
Northern	15,443
Yorks & Humber	15,003
North West	16,902
East Midlands	15,836
West Midlands	18,493
Wales	17,061
Scotland	19,371
Northern Ireland	21,824
United Kingdom	19,925

Source: Building Societies Association (1980)

In spite of these observations regarding population and employment structure, Devon has experienced some increase in the provision of employment in light manufacturing and processing, especially in Exeter and North Devon. This is probably due, at least in part, to the fact that this latter area is recognised for regional policy assistance.

Settlement pattern and housing provision in Devon

Apart from being located in one of the most expensive regions in Britain as far as house prices are concerned, Devon has a distinctive settlement pattern and also certain differences in tenure types from the national picture. The 1952 County Development Plan had provided large scale planning, mainly focused on Plymouth, Exeter and Torbay, although it did provide some initial recognition of the problems which can afflict rural areas, many of which have been touched on in chapter two. However, it was not until the first Review of the Development Plan (Devon County Council 1964) that any coherent basis for a rural settlement policy in Devon was established.

The First Review laid particular stress on the 'central place functions' which thriving rural communities should possess, such as public utilities, social facilities (schools, places of worship, possibly a GP's surgery), shops (for convenience goods), employment in the village or nearby, and adequate public transport services and roads. To create such thriving local communities, more positive coordinated public investment was envisaged than had previously been the case in order to maintain services and facilities and to ensure that new development would occur in the most appropriate places and that these would be in a supportive settlement system.

In particular, regional centres (Plymouth, Torbay, Exeter and Barnstaple) were designated, along with certain sub-urban towns and key inland and coastal towns, but, from a rural point of view, the selection of sixty-eight key settlements is of most interest. These were to be the only rural locations in which major extensions of residential development and public utilities were envisaged, and thus planners could justify discouraging development in other villages. This would also ensure minimum levels of services, particularly in areas with static or declining populations. The logic that this attitude might further encourage selective rural depopulation is, of course, only too obvious.

Rural industries, services, development and investment would therefore all be channelled into the key settlements. The Devon policy was thus to provide a comprehensive role for the settlements so designated. The Second Review (Devon County Council 1972) maintained largely the same policies regarding the settlement pattern and, as the County Structure Plan (Devon County Council 1979) states, the definition of key settlements was intended to take account of rural depopulation, but it was not anticipated that it necessarily would, or could, reverse the trend significantly. So, as described earlier, the north and west of the County continued to exhibit signs of population decline.

After the Second Review of the County Development Plan (in 1970), development in key settlements was felt to have been satisfactory and even to have retarded some rural population decline in north and central Devon. Some minor readjustments were made to the original sixty-eight settlements, with a net loss of three settlements overall. However, it is fairly certain that sixty-eight settlements spread countywide were too many to be guaranteed either growth or the range of public service provision envisaged in the policy (Cloke 1979).

With the reorganisation of local government in 1974, many previously fragmented public authorities became organised on similar spatial bases. Health services, education, transport and water authorities were unified and were thus presumably able to take a far broader strategic view of the range of settlements which they could all hope to serve. The three major urban areas of Exeter, Plymouth and Torbay came under the auspices of Devon County and, as a result, it may be suspected that a more realistic appraisal was made of settlement policy. In particular, the opportunity for 'new starts' and new strategies offered by structure planning has been seized by numerous authorities, not only Devon.

Rural decline is still noted as a cause for concern in the Devon Structure Plan (Devon County Council 1979) and, again, a solution is sought via a hierarchy of settlements, within which various levels of service can be provided or preserved, with a bottom tier guaranteed a range of services and transport links. Fewer settlements form the lower tier (even if it may be felt that there are still rather too many) and the settlement hierarchy now approved consists of four sub-regional centres, twenty-six area centres and thirty-eight 'selected local centres', instead of the sixty-eight key settlements of the old plans. The majority of these were, in fact, previously in the list of key settlements, although there were some minor adjustments. The locations of these settlements and comparisons with the previous hierarchy are shown in Figure 4.1. These selected local centres would be accorded ".... a priority in the provision of educational, social, health and postal services, outside Area or higher level centres ...." and would be provided with infrastructure to allow development on specified scales, certain acreages being allocated for residential and employment purposes in most centres (Devon County Council 1979, p.51).

Naturally, these thirty-eight selected local centres are spread more thinly on the ground than were the key settlements but they too meet certain service provision criteria. They meet (or will meet) at least six of the following requirements: possession of basic facilities (viz. primary school, post office, resident, or frequently visiting, doctor); eleven or more shops; dispensing chemist; bank; local employment in the parish of 100 or more jobs; daily bus service; place of worship, inn and village hall. These requirements do have some flexibility, however, and in the more remote settlements, a smaller number of shops (five or more) is acceptable instead of the eleven specified above. Nevertheless, settlements selected on the basis of these criteria will be of great importance in general levels of service provision, contributing considerably to the life of their surrounding areas, and they will be the foci for local development. Outside the Area Centres and Selected Local Centres, the extent to which residential development will be permitted may well be considerably restricted if the settlements possess 'character' which is considered worthy of retention. In many of these smaller settlements, only residential infilling and 'rounding off' will be permitted. Therefore, the settlement hierarchy adopted in the new structure plans promises to provide the blueprint for much of the physical and social development of the rural areas of the county for some time to come.

Development in Devon

Economic imbalance is clearly a problem in Devon since the three most important Sub-Regional Centres are located in the south of the County (at Exeter, Plymouth and Torbay). Up to 1976, the fourth Sub-Regional Centre of Barnstaple had grown at a comparatively slower rate. The economic growth of the main centres was accompanied by a lack of growth in many of the rural parts of the county, particularly the north and west, which experienced the outward flow of population described earlier, especially in the younger working age groups.

A major feature of economic imbalance in the County has been an uneven pressure on services and housing due to these differential economic growth rates which in the north and west have tended to be much lower than those in the south and east. This is partly a result of the major urban areas being in the south and east of the County with about half of Devon's population living in Plymouth, Torbay and Exeter. These centres have great importance as employment foci yet each possesses quite distinctive industrial mixes: in Plymouth, the dockyards; in Torbay, tourism; and, in Exeter, the service industries (particularly administration, education and the distributive trades) are important employers. As a result, they tend to be differentially vulnerable to varying economic conditions nationally.

The pressure of urban areas on the countryside for recreation, housing and services has naturally been greatest around these three main centres. Choices have often had to be made between conflicting uses for land, usually agriculture versus development. As the Devon County Council (1979) point out, many pressures are also created in settlements at some distance from but dependent upon the main centres. The result has been their need to expand physically and to provide services for residents, some of whom may commute to work in the main urban centres.

As an example, Figure 4.1 illustrates that South Hams falls between the influence of Plymouth in the west and Torbay in the east. This has created local pressures within parts of the South Hams as certain settlements (which will be discussed in more detail later) have been called upon to grow, at least in part, to serve these urban areas. The demands this has placed upon settlements such as Ivybridge will be a theme frequently referred to in the remainder of the book.

Rural decline has had a number of manifestations in Devon, many of which are similar to the general trends outlined in chapter two. Fewer job opportunities in the primary sector, the importance of which to Devon's employment structure was outlined previously, have encouraged outward migration from rural areas to local centres or even to urban areas outside the county altogether. There has been a tendency for a reduction of local services which can be attributed to a number of sometimes interrelated causes, such as the increase in car ownership which enables people to seek jobs and services (including shops) in a wider area than they could do otherwise. The corollary of this has been a reduction in public transport, exacerbating the plight of non-car owners or those without access to cars for daily service requirements. As identified in chapter two, services have often undergone what is viewed as 'rationalisation', which has usually meant a concentration of schools, medical and social services into larger settlements. This is, of course, in line with the officially sanctioned settlement policy. The net result can be increasing inconvenience to those living in smaller settlements who do not have ready access to private transport, for local services (shops in particular) have often closed, being unable to compete with larger scale urban counterparts.

Devon County Council (1979) suggests that this pattern of rural change may tend to disadvantage the elderly, school leavers and the less affluent rural dwellers. In addition, there may be pressure on some social services due to in-migration of retired persons, particularly to coastal areas in the south of the County which have clearly been identified as major targets for retirement migration (see, for example, Law and Warnes 1976). The location of the major retirement destinations in the County has similarities to the location of tourism although the latter is rather more widespread, with foci in coastal resorts such as Teignmouth, Dawlish, Exmouth, Paignton and Torquay, but also spreading into the National Park areas within the County. It will be evident again that the majority of these tourist resorts are in the southern part of the County which, coupled with its generally higher levels of economic development, has resulted in most transport improvements serving this area rather than the north and west.

In terms of transport, the county is now much better served by main road links than in the 1960s, especially since the M5 motorway reached Exeter in 1975. The county structure plan strategy reflects the economic advantages that have followed the completion of the M5/A38 trunk road to Plymouth, and the A30 and A38 links between Devon and the South and South East of England are also important. In the centre of the county, the A30 west of Exeter is undergoing improvements towards Okehampton, and the accessibility of the northern reaches of the county will eventually be improved by the proposed North Devon Link to Barnstaple and Bideford. Rail transport also plays its part as Exeter and Plymouth have benefited from the new high speed Inter-City links with the rest of Britain.

The county strategy thus acknowledges that the major potential of Devon will lie in the main urban centres which are, or will be, served by this major road and communications network. This is strongly related to the differential growth rates (and growth potential) throughout various areas of the county referred to in the earlier pages of this chapter. The inevitable result must be a further polarisation of the county into favoured and less favoured areas, with an increase of pressure on those settlements well served by main transport routes to the detriment of the poorly served settlements.

Housing in Devon

In 1975 there was a total stock of some 346,000 dwellings in Devon (an increase of 31 per cent or 81,700 dwellings on the 1961 figure). 46 per cent of the total stock was situated in the three main urban areas of Plymouth, Torbay and Exeter. The patterns of tenure in Devon compared with England and Wales can be illustrated as in Table 4.3, from which the nationally observed increase in owner-occupancy and decline in private rental can also be seen to have occurred in the county.

These figures illustrate that, nationally, a decline in private rented accommodation has been compensated, to some extent, by an increase in local authority housing provision. However, no such compensation has occurred in Devon, where a 10 per cent fall in privately rented dwellings has only been accompanied by a 1 per cent increase in local authority housing. It may be surprising that a county such as Devon, identified earlier as having considerable proportions of residents in 'low wage' occupations, should lag behind the national average in provision of local authority housing. If the large urban settlements of Plymouth and Exeter are discounted, an even more uneven picture of local authority participation in housing amongst the various districts of Devon is clearly evident (Table 4.4). Of the rural districts, only Tiverton, with 27 per cent of its housing stock owned by the council, approaches the national average; elsewhere, proportions of under 20 per cent are common.

Table 4.3
Distribution of households by tenure

	Percentages	
	1961	1971
Devon		
Owner–occupied	47	56
Local authority rented	20	21
Privately rented	33	23
Total	100	100

England and Wales		
Owner–occupied	42	50
Local authority rented	24	28
Privately rented	34	22
Total	100	100

Source: Devon County Council (1977)

The converse is, naturally, that high rates of owner–occupancy are to be seen, particularly in districts such as Torbay and East Devon, which are favoured for retirement or the migration of higher income groups. Considerable proportions remain in the private rented sector, illustrating a pattern which is explained by the tourist and second home type of functions of some of the areas. Second homes are, in fact, a relatively important feature of the county's housing.

The South West Economic Planning Council (1975) defined second homes as being ".... predominantly used by their owners rather than let on a series of short tenancies and sufficiently permanent in structure to be identified as separate rateable hereditaments ....". Table 4.5 illustrates the position of the districts of Devon with regard to second home ownership. These are almost certainly underestimates and, with some 1.1 per cent of housing stock known to be in use as second homes, this feature of the County's housing is certainly of importance. It may be seen that South Hams as a district has the highest proportion of second homes in Devon, accounting for approximately one-third of the total, which is of significance since the district forms the study area for this book.

Table 4.4
Household tenure by districts in Devon, 1971

| District | Percentages | | | |
	Owner-occupied	Local authority rented	Private rented	Total
East Devon	61	17	22	100
Exeter	55	25	20	100
North Devon	61	16	23	100
Plymouth	45	30	25	100
South Hams	55	19	26	100
Teignbridge	60	17	23	100
Tiverton	49	27	24	100
Torbay	66	12	22	100
Torridge	61	16	23	100
West Devon	58	15	27	100
Devon	56	21	23	100

Source: Devon County Council (1977)

Table 4.5
Proportion of second homes in the housing stock

District	Percentage of second homes in housing stock	No. of second homes
Torridge	2.0	355
North Devon	1.7	470
West Devon	0.9	130
Tiverton	0.4	85
Teignbridge	0.8	290
Exeter	0.0	0
East Devon	1.4	580
Plymouth	0.0	0
South Hams	4.5	1,135
Torbay	0.9	405
Devon	1.1	3,450

Source: adapted from draft SHDC district plan

SOUTH HAMS: A RURAL DISTRICT IN A RURAL COUNTY

The location of the main case study on which this book is based is the district administered by the South Hams District Council (SHDC). This is the administrative name for a long recognised geographical area although the precise boundaries have been a matter for some debate in the past. There is considerable historical evidence of its uncertain boundaries and Saville (1957, p.172) cites the example of the late eighteenth century writer Robert Fraser who discussed the possible definitions of the area:

> ".... different opinions are held respecting the bounds of that part of the district called the South Hams, some stating it to be that part south of the Dart, and others to extend to the river Ex; but by the best informed, I find it strictly bounded by the river Teign, preceding up the Teign as far as Teign Bridge ... taking a line from Teign Bridge to the south part of (Bovey Heathfield) it proceeds as before described, along the south of the Dartmoor hills to Plymouth, including a tract of county nearly equal to one-fourth part of the whole county, and in point of richness of soil, abundance of grain, fruit and sheep, perhaps not equalled by any district of similar extent in Great Britain ...."

Later authors tended to restrict the South Hams to smaller areas, usually to the southern fringes of Dartmoor from Tavistock in the west to the Teign in the east. Saville's own survey parishes were located within the boundaries of lines drawn from Totnes to Ivybridge, Ivybridge to Kingsbridge and Kingsbridge to the Dart Estuary just north of Dartmouth. This was therefore a more tightly constrained area than is currently administered by SHDC, the area of this study.

Physically and scenically, the district is extremely pleasant. It has an equable climate, with mild winters and very varied rainfall, from about 35 inches per annum in the south-east to about 60 inches in the parishes which are located on the Dartmoor slopes. It is certainly a rural part of Devon on Cloke's index although it does have a number of important settlements and has the major A38 trunk road Plymouth to Exeter running through it. This brings rapid transport through the district and the A38/M5 link to the Midlands has opened up the area considerably for motor-borne tourist activity.

The history of the development of the South Hams District Council is important as background to the remainder of the book because it has, to an extent, influenced the nature of housing provision in various parts of the Council's district. It was one of the new councils formed in the 1974 reorganisation of local government and, as constituted, it comprised parts of a number of other authorities. The two main county constituencies of which SHDC was formed were parts of Tavistock CC and Totnes CC. There were also three rural districts of Plympton St Mary RD, Totnes RD and Kingsbridge RD, with two urban

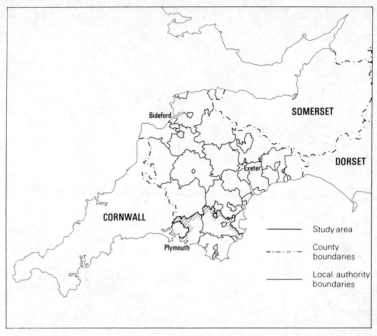

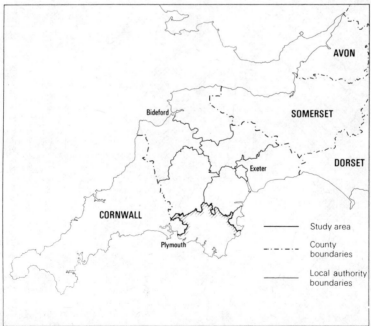

Figure 4.2: Local government in Devon before (upper diagram)
and after (lower diagram) reorganisation   1974

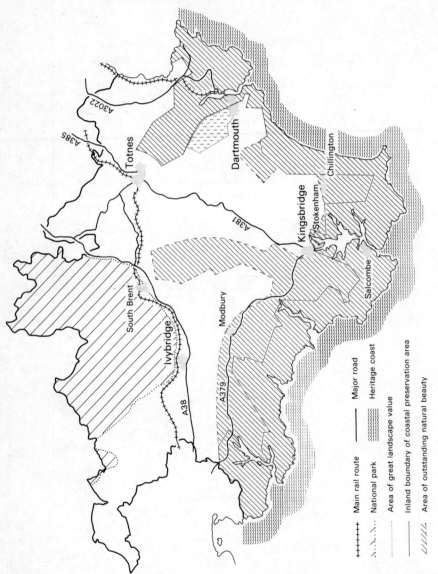

Figure 4.3: Settlement pattern in South Hams 1979
Source: after Devon County Council (1979)

Legend:

++++++ Main rail route

.·.·.·. National park

///// Area of great landscape value

········ Inland boundary of coastal preservation area

///// Area of outstanding natural beauty

———— Major road

///// Heritage coast

Map labels: A3022, A385, Totnes, Dartmouth, Chillington, Kingsbridge, Stokenham, A381, Salcombe, South Brent, Modbury, Ivybridge, A379, A38 districts of Kingsbridge UD and Salcombe UD. Finally, the two municipal boroughs of Totnes MB and Dartmouth MB were also included in the new district. Thus, a considerable variety of local government units were incorporated into the new District, as illustrated in Figure 4.2. It may be seen that, in the east, boundary changes have resulted in part of Brixham UD being transferred to the parish of Kingswear and the parish of Churston Ferrers joining Torbay County Borough. To the west there were also some adjustments as Plymouth CB took in parts of the old Plympton St Mary and Plymstock parishes. The northern boundaries of SHDC remained those of the old Plympton St Mary and Totnes Rural Districts.

This administrative history has resulted in a variety of proportions of housing tenures being inherited by SHDC, which will be discussed more fully in chapter five. Prior to this, however, the population, settlement and employment settings in the South Hams will be outlined, as a background for the following empirical chapters. The area which has been formed is fairly heterogeneous although there are a number of moderately large centres. However, none is really large enough to provide a central focus for the District which has, as a result, a some-what fragmented social and economic character.

Settlement and constraints on development

Figure 4.1 illustrates the settlement hierarchy for Devon, showing the position in 1972 and 1979. The more detailed Figure 4.3 shows the current picture in the South Hams, and also indicates a number of local constraints on development, namely the Dartmoor National Park, the south coast Area of Outstanding Natural Beauty, the coastal preservation area and the heritage coast. The figure also clearly illustrates the major settlements which dominate the South Hams: Plymouth in the west and Torbay in the east, with Totnes, Dartmouth, Ivybridge and Kingsbridge being the main local settlements. Modbury, Salcombe, South Brent and Stokenham/Chillington are designated as Selected Local Centres in the 1979 Devon County Council Structure Plan and, as such, will be accorded the development and service priorities outlined earlier in the chapter.

The population of the SHDC area was 59,898 in 1971, with 66,980 estimated for mid-1976 and a 1981 census figure of 67,900. Of the sixty-two parishes comprising the district, seventeen lost population between 1961 and 1978, the most substantial taking place in the moorland fringe parishes such as Holne and West Buckfastleigh and in isolated estuaries and coastal locations such as Dittisham (see Figure 4.4, and parish names may be seen in Figure 4.5). The 1971 populations, with 1976 estimates and 1981 projections are given for the largest parishes in Table 4.6; however, at the time of writing, parish populations for 1981 were not available. The major population increases in this period took place in the settlements from which commuting to Torbay or Plymouth was possible, for example, Ivybridge, Wembury, Kingswear and Berry Pomeroy, and in popular retirement

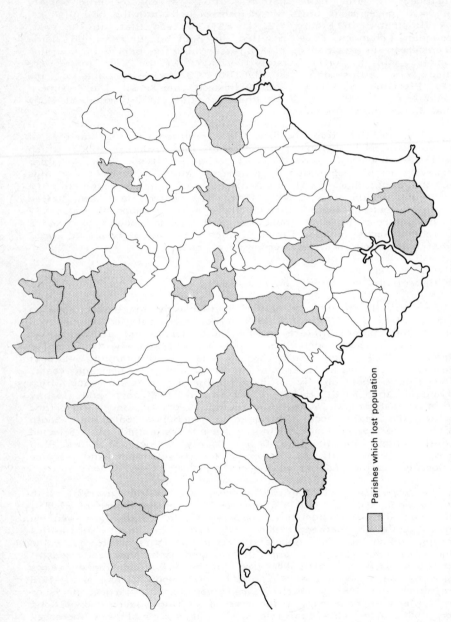

Figure 4.4: South Hams: parishes losing population 1961–1978
Source: after draft SHDC district plan

☐ Parishes which lost population

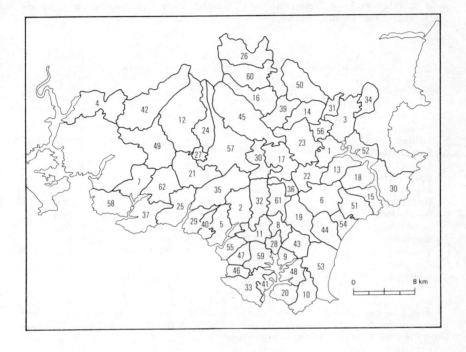

1	Ashprington	22	Halwell	42	Shaugh Prior
2	Aveton Gifford	23	Harberton	43	Sherford
3	Berry Pomeroy	24	Harford	44	Slapton
4	Bickleigh	25	Holbeton	45	S. Brent
5	Bigbury	26	Holne	46	S. Huish
6	Blackawton	27	Ivybridge	47	S. Milton
7	Brixton	28	Kingsbridge	48	S. Pool
8	Buckland	29	Kingston	49	Sparkwell
9	Charleton	30	Kingswear	50	Staverton
10	Chivelstone	31	Littlehempston	51	Stoke Fleming
11	Churchstow	32	Loddiswell	52	Stoke Gabriel
12	Cornwood	33	Malborough	53	Stokenham
13	Cornworthy	34	Marldon	54	Street
14	Dartington	35	Modbury	55	Thurlestone
15	Dartmouth	36	Morleigh	56	Totnes
16	Dean Prior	37	Newton Ferrers	57	Ugborough
17	Diptford		& Noss Mayo	58	Wembury
18	Dittisham	38	N. Huish	59	W. Alvington
19	E. Allington	39	Rattery	60	W. Buckfastleigh
20	E. Portlemouth	40	Ringmore	61	Woodleigh
21	Ermington	41	Salcombe	62	Yealmpton

Figure 4.5: South Hams: parish names and locations

areas such as Churchstow and Charleton. During this period, the previous major decline of inland, agricultural parishes was apparently arrested and only two parishes, East Portlemouth and Littlehempston, decreased by more than 10 per cent between 1971 and 1978 (Figure 4.5).

Table 4.6
South Hams : populations of main settlements

Settlement	1971 Census	1976 estimate	1981 Projection
Dartmouth	5,707	6,160	6,140
Kingsbridge	3,545	3,890	4,280
Totnes	5,772	6,020	5,950
Salcombe	2,496	3,180	3,120
Ivybridge	3,074	3,630	5,480
Dartington	1,560	1,590	1,650
Kingswear	1,301	1,520	1,560
Marldon	1,714	1,890	1,820
South Brent	1,876	1,950	2,090
Ugborough	2,096	2,110	2,620
Wembury	2,062	2,830	2,870
Yealmpton	1,220	1,600	1,740

Sources: 1971 Census; South Hams District Council.

The larger towns have continued to grow and are of great importance for the future of the district. Of the four Area Centres in the 1979 County Strategy for the District, Kingsbridge and Ivybridge have been identified as settlements which will be important for the provision of homes and jobs. In the last named, sixty acres of land have been designated for employment development and the Lee Mill area is now an important source of local employment, although Ivybridge itself is very much a 'village into town' (Glyn-Jones 1977), providing for commuters to Plymouth along the A38. Smaller areas of about ten acres each have been designated for employment development at Totnes, Kingsbridge and Dartmouth. Their continued expansion is to be expected, along with that of relatively affluent commuter villages such as Yealmpton, Wembury, and Brixton, all of which give their names to parishes and the two last named in particular having considerable proportions (over 30 per cent) of their economically active populations in managerial and professional employment.

Economic activity in the South Hams

An examination of Table 4.7 illustrates the importance (even if declining) of primary activity to the employment structure of the South Hams District. The employment in construction is also declining although service employment, including shops, hotels and central and local government, is increasing in importance and almost two-thirds of the workforce are now in this

62

sector. Service industry employment traditionally gives greater stability to a locality but it should be noted that a considerable proportion of the service employment in South Hams tends to be related to the tourist industry and hence is seasonal and more susceptible to the fluctuations and vagaries of the national economy. Accurate information on employment in tourism is notoriously difficult to obtain due to the seasonal and casual nature of much of the work. In June 1976, the SHDC produced a rough estimate of 1500 people employed in the hotel and catering sectors (excluding the self-employed), out of a 1976 employed population of some 17,800. The employment in support services, such as retailing, transport and distribution, which are indirectly dependent on tourism, is, of course, even harder to assess. However, SHDC estimate that the numbers employed in tourism and related industries appear to be similar to those in agriculture.

Table 4.7
Employment structure in the South Hams

	South Hams				Devon
	1971		1976		1976
Industrial Sector	No.	Percentage	No.	Percentage	
Agriculture, fishing, forestry	1,483	9.3	1,322	7.4)	4.3
Mining and quarrying	300	1.9	269	1.6)	
Manufacturing	2,722	17.1	2,846	15.9	22.0
Construction	2,089	13.1	1,897	10.6	7.4
Services	9,349	58.6	11,512	64.5	66.3
Total	15,943	100.0	17,846	100.0	100.0

Source: Department of Employment and draft SHDC district plan

Table 4.7 also indicates a slight decline in manufacturing employment plus a more marked decline in agricultural employment between 1971 and 1976, with service employment growing in importance. However, figures for agricultural employment do vary according to the source, and Ministry of Agriculture statistics suggest that agricultural employment is not as low as the Department of Employment's figures indicate, because these returns do not include the self-employed and the various family members involved in farming. The Ministry of Agriculture census data probably give a rather more accurate overall picture of the real employment in agriculture, and, at 2,058, are almost 60 per cent higher than the Department of Employment's figures.

In considering the economic and social conditions in any district, at least some mention should be made of rates of car ownership, particularly in view of the declining availability of public transport. Somewhat surprisingly, Devon as a whole has higher rates of car ownership or availability than the rest of England and Wales. Perhaps this is because, in spite of relatively low earned incomes, the rural nature of the county influences many people to regard the possession of a car as a necessity. This suggestion does appear to have some substance as, in 1971, only about 30 per cent of households in most rural districts lacked a car, compared to 47 per cent in the urban areas of Devon. The South Hams itself follows this pattern, as illustrated in Table 4.8, for over half of its households have access to one car, whilst over 12 per cent have two or more available.

Table 4.8
Car ownership rates :
England and Wales, Devon, South Hams
(1971)

| | Percentage of households owning: | | | |
	No car	1 car	2 (or more)	Total
England and Wales	48	44	8	100
Devon	43	47	10	100
South Hams District	36	51.5	12.5	100

Source: Devon County Council (1977)

The importance of car ownership rates is highlighted if the actual locations of employment in the district are considered. This is now examined in the following section.

Location of major employment opportunities The location of the main employment opportunities in an area is of major importance to any study of housing as this will influence journey to work patterns, transport needs and the chances of obtaining work locally. The following section paints a picture of the location of the major employers, and the chapters which come later in the book will make use of this background in assessing housing need and demand.

First, employment in agriculture (which accounts for, possibly, 12 per cent of the employed population), is naturally the most widespread in the South Hams. It does, however, have major significance in the southern SHDC area, centred on the Kingsbridge Employment Office, where some 15 per cent of workers are involved in agriculture, fishing and forestry. This falls to only 3 per cent in the western area office of Plympton near Plymouth. Elsewhere, farming employment is relatively widely scattered with foci around the main settlements but of special importance in the area south of a line approximately from Plymouth to Dartmouth, where land is classified mainly as grades 1 and 2, or grade 3 at worst.

Tourism also enjoys a fairly wide spread, although being focused around the settlements such as Totnes where bed-and-breakfast and tourist-related service employment is to be found. However, the majority of tourist developments have a coastal orientation, with over two-thirds of the total employed estimated to be in the Dartmouth and Kingsbridge areas. A certain spin-off from the major tourist area of Torbay naturally occurs in the eastern reaches of the South Hams, although the quantitative and qualitative effects of this are very difficult to estimate. It probably takes the form of some demand for labour from Torbay in the eastern parts of South Hams whilst some local services and tourist attractions in Totnes, Dartington, Kingswear and Slapton feel the impact of day visitors from nearby Torbay.

Employment, other than that generated in connection with the tourist industry, is mainly provided in services especially by public bodies, with the District Council itself being a major employer, mainly at its Totnes headquarters. Other public employers include the Devon County Council (schools, police, fire services, social services and the like); the health service with NHS hospitals at Totnes, Dartmouth, Kingsbridge, Lee Mill and Moorhaven; and central government with some employment in defence, the Forestry Commission, the Department of Health and Social Security and the like. Dartmouth is, of course, a major focus of employment in the armed forces; and the Royal Naval training college provides a considerable focus for local employment in ancillary jobs. However, public sector employment is by and large concentrated in the main towns of Totnes, Dartmouth, Kingsbridge and Ivybridge.

There is a tendency to discount manufacturing as a major employer in an area like that of SHDC. However, scattered small manufacturing and craft works aside, there are now a number of important locations for manufacturing within the District. In general, manufacturing activities are concentrated at the Lee Mill Industrial Estate near Ivybridge and at Totnes, although there are some small firms located at Staverton, Kingswear and Dartmouth.

Unemployment Finally, mention must be made of the problems facing people in search of employment in the district as this will emphasise the relatively small choice which presents itself to individuals in any local area. Unemployment rates have consistently been above the national rates for the country as a whole and also above the rates for the county of Devon. For example, in 1977, February unemployment rates for Dartmouth Employment Office area were 14.2 per cent, compared with 8.4 per cent in Devon and 5.9 per cent in the UK. July unemployment in that year was 10.9 per cent in Dartmouth, 8.4 per cent in Devon and 6.7 per cent in UK. Figures for January 1979 were Dartmouth 12.6 per cent and Devon 8.5 per cent, falling in July 1979 to 10.6 per cent in Dartmouth and 7.1 per cent in Devon as a whole.

A more gloomy outlook greets locals who are seeking employment and, as ever, the young and unskilled fare particularly badly in the tight employment market. The true extent of unemployment, underemployment and 'hidden' unemployment, particularly amongst women, for whom there are very few opportunities, is very difficult to gauge. This is particularly worrying in the category of hidden unemployment amongst school leavers who may often leave the district for other areas of the country. Many who go on to complete further and higher education also find that local jobs are not available to suit their skills and they may well be forced to become part of the exodus to more promising employment opportunities in urban areas. Those who want a good career structure frequently have to migrate and this, of course, can be a very depressing social trend for a rural district, which can become denuded of its most talented and imaginative residents. Cohort studies in the South Hams have backed up this contention that there has been persistent out-migration of younger aged persons and in-migration of people in the older age groups. Of the 426 children aged 0 - 4 in 1951 in Totnes, 417 were expected to be alive in 1971 (aged 20 - 24) but, in fact, only 350 were present, indicating an outward movement of 16 per cent. There is reason to believe that such a trend is continuing in the SHDC and may well gather momentum as the recession further reduces local employment opportunities.

South Hams - an overview

The impression remains of a rural district, well endowed with agricultural resources and excellent natural scenery for tourism. The casual visitor may well be excused for feeling a twinge of jealousy of local residents who seem to have a most pleasant environment in which to live. However, on closer inspection, not all is so pleasant. Employment opportunities are generally poor, wages are low and accessibility is also poor at the district level. The 'growth centres' such as Totnes, Ivybridge and Kingsbridge may well be foci for internal migration but some are also foci for commuters and for retired persons. The local community may feel little in common with them whilst a degree of gentrification in the towns may push up housing prices, putting them beyond the reach of locals. The choices that are available within the South Hams for prospective home owners or tenants are extremely important and, as discussed in chapters two and three, housing is a fundamental matter for all, especially when incomes are low and problems of accessibility high. The following chapter is therefore devoted to an examination of the nature and location of housing in the SHDC area with a particular reference to the role of the public sector in the housing market.

5 Housing in the South Hams

This chapter now looks at the local housing circumstances in the study area covered by South Hams District Council. It is divided into sections, the first of which deals with the overall housing stock in the South Hams and the proportions of housing in the different tenures. The sections following this concentrate on the local authority sector of the housing market, and the location and type of its housing stock.

HOUSING LOCATION AND TENURE

The SHDC which, it will be recalled from chapter four, came into being in 1974, inherited a geographical area from the previous local authorities which contained the full range of housing tenure types seen nationally. At the time of the 1971 Census, the housing stock of the area now covered by SHDC was comprised of 54.7 per cent owner-occupied households, 18.7 per cent local authority rented and 26.6 per cent privately rented. In chapter four, the corresponding figures for the County of Devon were seen to be 56 per cent owner-occupied, 21 per cent local authority rented and 23 per cent privately rented. The SHDC was therefore somewhat below the County average in owner occupancy and local authority rental rates but slightly above its level for private rental. Of course, the SHDC, as was also true of Devon as a whole, was considerably below the national figure of 28 per cent for local authority provision of housing.

The location of these main tenure types within the South Hams can be mapped as in Figure 5.1 and this presents quite an interesting picture. It is clear that the main concentrations of owner-occupied housing are to be found in the better off parishes, those which have higher proportions of their residents engaged in managerial and professional occupations and those with higher proportions of retired people. Figure 5.2 shows the former to be located mainly in the west, with some near to coastal areas and in parishes from which large numbers of people commute to Plymouth, such as Wembury, Newton and Noss, Ivybridge, Brixton and Ermington. At the 1971 Census, all of these parishes had at least 55 per cent of their housing stocks in the hands of owner occupiers, and in some this proportion was as high as 81 per cent. The retirement areas, mentioned in chapter four, display similar high rates, as found in Stokenham (69 per cent owner-occupied), Slapton (67 per cent), Malborough (75 per cent), Bigbury (64 per cent) and Charleton (72 per cent).

At the other extreme, a number of parishes have very low rates of owner-occupancy, especially those to the north of

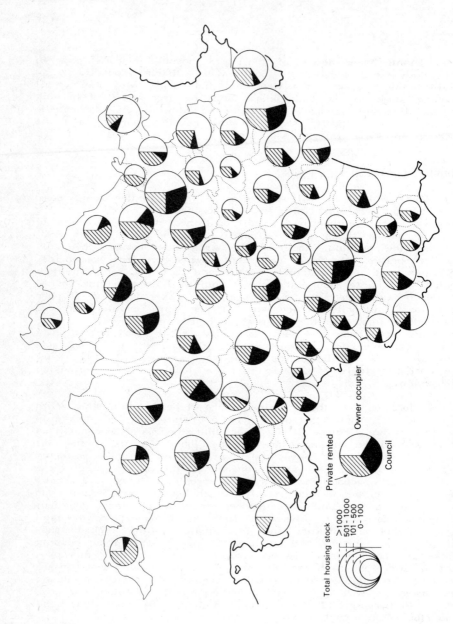

Figure 5.1: Housing tenure 1971
Source: 1971 Census

Owner occupier

Private rented

Council

Total housing stock

>1000
501-1000
101-500
0-100

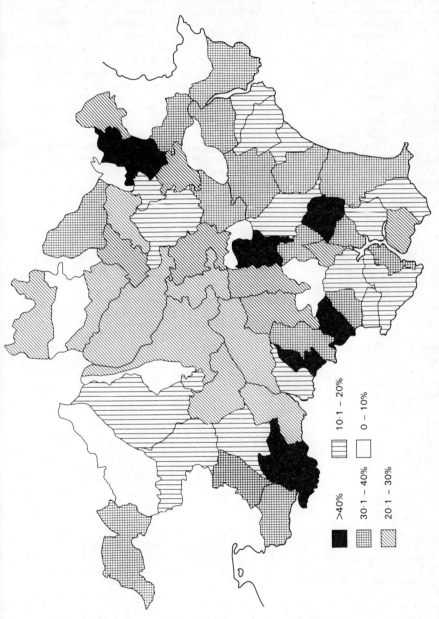

Figure 5.2: Employers, managers and professional persons as a
proportion of economically active population 1971
Source: 1971 Census

10·1 – 20%

0 – 10%

>40%

30·1 – 40%

20·1 – 30%

Plymouth, such as Bickleigh (23 per cent owner–occupancy) and Shaugh Prior (27 per cent) and some of the northern parishes on the Dartmoor fringe. By way of compensation, these parishes tend to have considerable proportions of their housing stock let as private rentals, possibly due to the influence of holiday home ownership, which will be discussed more fully in the following pages. Parishes such as Holne and West Buckfastleigh have about one–third of their housing stock privately rented, and a similar pattern is to be seen in an even more extreme form in some of the upper Dart Valley parishes such as Staverton (58 per cent privately rented), Dartington (46 per cent) and Littlehempston (44 per cent). Both owner–occupancy and local authority rental sectors are accordingly much smaller in most of these parishes. Some anxiety must be expressed about the physical fabric of some of these privately rented houses, because lack of fitness tends to be found more commonly in this tenure than in the other two main forms of tenure, as the national figures cited in Table 5.1 adequately illustrate.

Table 5.1
Unfitness and lack of amenities by tenure :
England and Wales, 1976

Percentages of stock in each tenure

	Owner–occupied	Local authority rented	Other (mainly private rented)	All Tenures
Unfit dwellings	3.0	1.0	16.0	5.0
No fixed bath	3.0	1.0	17.0	5.0
No inside WC	4.0	3.0	19.0	9.0
Lacking one or more basic amenities	5.0	6.0	26.0	9.0
Total	100.0	100.0	100.0	100.0
(All dwellings in tenure, in thousands)	(10125)	(5067)	(2444)	(18133)

Source : after Lansley (1979)

The distribution of local authority owned houses may also be briefly outlined although, by itself, this feature is not of great interest for it is other facets such as age, size and type of dwelling which can be of greater significance for residents and would-be residents; these will be considered more fully later. In terms of proportions of the overall housing stock, the main concentrations of local authority dwellings are clearly in the major settlements in the South Hams: 29.8 per cent of the housing stock in Totnes was local authority owned in 1971, with 23.8 per cent in Kingsbridge and 27.4 per cent in Dartmouth. Other high proportions (although numerically less important)

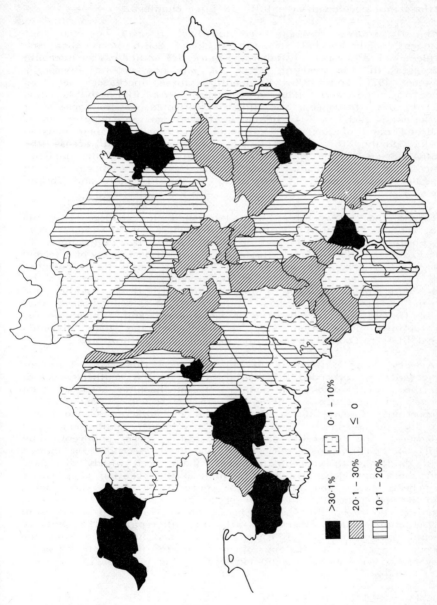

Figure 5.3: Percentage change in housing stock 1971–1979
Source: after draft SHDC district plan

>30·1%

20·1 – 30%

10·1 – 20%

0·1 – 10%

≤ 0

may be seen in the parishes of Dean Prior, Loddiswell, South Brent and Yealmpton. The implications of concentration into the main urban settlements will be considered in the following sections and developed more fully in later chapters.

If all tenures are examined together, it may be seen that changes in the overall housing stock of South Hams show the influence of a number of factors. Figure 5.3 indicates considerable increases in the housing stock of parishes around Plymouth, between 1971 and 1979. Frequently, these increases were as large as one-third. Housing pressure from Plymouth is thus clearly one influence, and this is reflected in the growth of settlements such as Ivybridge, alluded to in chapter four. A broad band of parishes experiencing increases in their housing stocks during this period is to be seen running across the central areas of the South Hams, possibly reflecting the parishes nearest to major trunk roads which have experienced housing pressure as a result of commuting to the Plymouth and Torbay areas.

Second home ownership was mentioned in chapter four as one important feature of the housing stock of the South West of England in general and of Devon and the South Hams in particular. Figure 5.4 illustrates the importance of second homes as a proportion of housing stock in South Hams parishes for 1973, based on a survey of second homes undertaken by the South West Economic Planning Council. It is likely, due to the difficulties of precise enumeration of second homes, that these figures are considerable underestimates and, unfortunately, no definite information was recorded for the then Plympton Rural District Council area in the west of what is now SHDC.

A very clear pattern is to be seen from this map. The preponderance of recorded second homes is in the southern coastal parishes, with almost one-quarter of the housing stock of East Portlemouth recorded as being in use as second homes in 1973. Proportions of over 10 to 15 per cent of stock as second homes are to be seen in South Pool, Chivelstone, Malborough and Salcombe. The inherent dangers (possibly more apparent than real) of housing large numbers of non-local, second home owners with dwellings in concentrated areas have been widely discussed and these are generally felt to include the creation of pressure on cheap local housing and the generation of a very fickle and irregular demand for local shops and services. The converse may be, however, that second homes do at least help to maintain stock that would otherwise fall into disrepair. The balance of this argument is, of course, very hard to gauge, but the second home is a feature of housing in this district which may create some extra demand for local authority houses.

LOCAL AUTHORITY INVOLVEMENT

When the South Hams District Council came into being in 1974, there was no single body in charge of public housing across the geographical area for which it became responsible. Prior

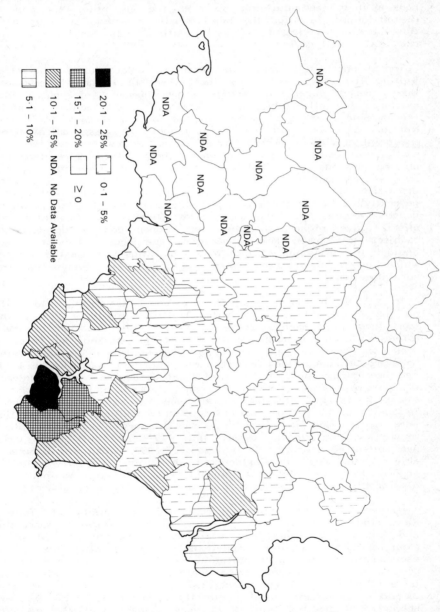

Figure 5.4: Second homes as a proportion of housing stock 1973
Source: unpublished data, South West Economic Planning Council

20·1 – 25%   0·1 – 5%

15·1 – 20%   ≥ 0

10·1 – 15%   NDA No Data Available

5·1 – 10%

to this date, local authority housing had been dealt with by various departments within each of the many local government units which were to make up SHDC. In particular, the SHDC found that a considerable backlog of demand for local authority housing had been building up over the years to 1974 and it seemed appropriate for the new council to attempt to deal with this backlog (reflected in long waiting lists for housing) in such ways as it could.

The Council felt that, in order to clear quite substantial waiting lists in a relatively short time, fairly drastic measures were needed purely to bring larger numbers of houses into existence for allocation. As a result, it was decided to build considerable numbers of houses in the four main towns of Totnes, Kingsbridge, Dartmouth and Ivybridge. It was logical from the point of view of deriving scale economies and, hence, reducing costs, that estates should be built, whether these were desirable on the grounds of distribution of demand or desirable socially and environmentally. The advantages of estate building were discussed in chapter three, and Shucksmith (1981) writes that generally, part of the reason for the building of larger, higher density estates was the government subsidy system which, in effect, gave higher subsidies for higher density developments (subject to Parker Morris minimum standards). This militated against the provision of individual dwellings and smaller estates which might have been more appropriate in many scattered rural locations.

In the South Hams, plans progressed quite smoothly to build up the stock of local authority dwellings in three out of the four large settlements, although whether the location of these estates was appropriate with regard to demand for housing does not seem to have been fully considered. In Dartmouth, however, although the land on which houses were to be built had been determined, a degree of local opposition was encountered when some conservationist interests claimed that the proposed estate would be intrusive in an amenity and recreation area. In addition, the proposed site was steeply inclined and difficulties were experienced in devising a satisfactory development plan, which was not finally passed until 1979. By this date, costs per unit were estimated to be about £25,000, which was unacceptable to the council. Furthermore, by this time, it could be argued that the political climate was changing against such a large direct local authority investment in housing provision.

However, in the other three main settlements of Totnes, Kingsbridge and Ivybridge, plans were generally successful and Figure 5.5 illustrates very convincingly the way in which local authority housing completions progressed after the initial decision to proceed with building. In 1976-1977, a large number of new houses appeared for allocation by SHDC and this timing is an important matter, elaborated in chapter eight. The main locations of these local authority completions 1976-1979 are shown in Table 5.2 and it is very evident that the majority are in the three main centres mentioned.

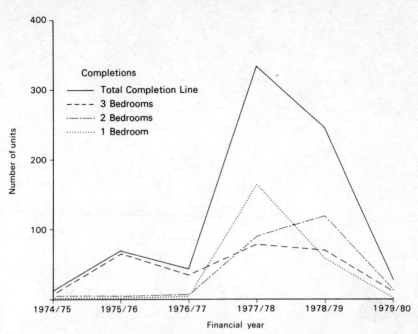

Figure 5.5: Local authority dwellings completed and bedroom numbers 1974–1980
Source: after draft SHDC district plan

Table 5.2
Public sector housing completions 1976–9

Parish	Number of completions
Brixton	46
Ermington	22
Ivybridge	88
Yealmpton	30
Dartmouth Town	54
Totnes Town	230
Kingsbridge Town	213
All other parishes	51
Total	734

Source: see Appendix A

Almost three-quarters of completions were therefore in the three main towns of Kingsbridge, Totnes and Ivybridge. Figure 5.5 also illustrates that, at this time, a considerable emphasis was being given to the provision of one-bedroom dwellings, and a number of the flat/maisonette/bungalow type were, in fact, intended for occupation by elderly persons. Of the total 734 completions plotted, some 212 (29 per cent) were designated for use as accommodation for the elderly and this feature is further considered in the following section when

75

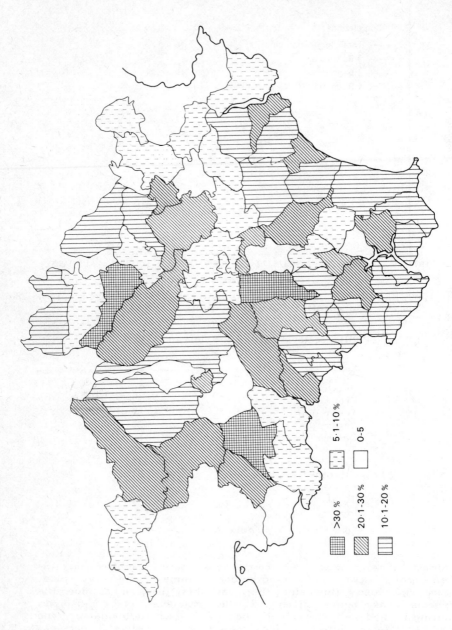

Figure 5.6: Percentage of housing stock in local authority ownership 1971
Source: 1971 Census

>30 %

20·1-30 %

10·1-20 %

5·1-10 %

0-5

the type and size of the housing stock and special housing characteristics are considered.

Finally, the present day structure of the administration of SHDC housing must be mentioned to indicate the advances that have been made in housing management locally. The impression of fragmentation of responsibility for housing post-1974 remains until 1979 when a separate Housing Department was established. Since then, an even more coordinated policy has been developed, with a Chief Housing Officer (now Director of Housing) in charge of this department, based at the Totnes Headquarters of SHDC.

In more recent years, there has been very little building by the council itself, partially as a result of financial strin- gencies imposed by central government, and this reduction in building is adequately illustrated in Figure 5.5. The Housing Department in SHDC, as in many other areas in Britain, has therefore undergone some role substitution, undertaking more varied activities such as cooperation with private developers and housing associations. The high council completion rates of 1977 are unlikely to be repeated and so allocations have increasingly become concerned with re-letting vacant dwellings rather than letting new ones.

CHARACTERISTICS OF LOCAL AUTHORITY HOUSING

Figure 5.6 illustrates the across-district distribution of local authority housing in the South Hams. Such data give a somewhat limited impression as they do not take account of variations in population densities but the map does show that only three parishes, Woodleigh, Harford and Littlehempston, are totally without local authority houses. This is a far more equitable picture than that found in the Lake District National Park, where twenty-nine out of eighty parishes were totally devoid of local authority houses (Shucksmith 1981). However, the South Hams, as a District under housing pressure, had a total local authority stock of only some 4,600 dwellings of all types in 1979, a total diminishing as sales proceed, as discussed in chapter eight. All that Figure 5.6 really indicates is the con- centration of housing in the main settlements, which point has been made previously and will be returned to. The new, post- 1974 construction, in particular, is concentrated in these settle- ments.

Of considerable interest as an element in the housing stock is the location of housing or accommodation for the elderly. There were some 290 dwelling units in what may be generally classed as 'sheltered accommodation' in the South Hams in early 1980; these included 161 bungalows, 111 flats and 18 bed-sitting rooms. In addition, some 508 places existed in 1970 in designated old people's properties. There were differences, however, in the distribution of these with the west of what is now SHDC relatively well provided, as shown in Figure 5.7. This is in part because the old Plympton Rural District had been particularly active in this aspect of housing provision.

77

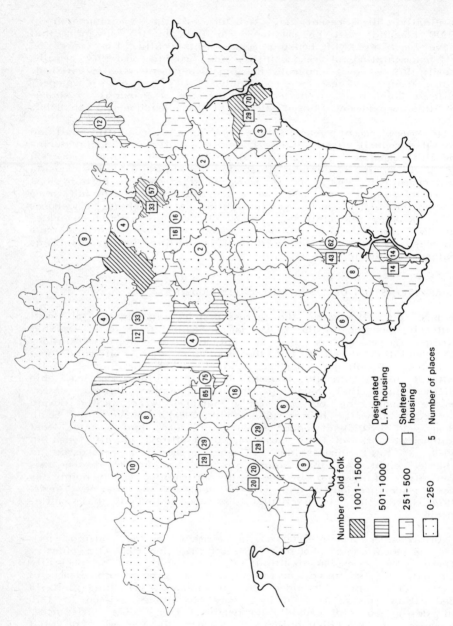

Figure 5.7: Housing provision for the elderly
Source: Appendix A

Number of old folk

▨ 1001 - 1500
▤ 501 - 1000
▯ 251 - 500
∴ 0 - 250

○ Designated L.A. housing
□ Sheltered housing
⑤ Number of places

Brixton, Yealmpton and Sparkwell have good proportions of both sheltered housing and local authority old people's housing. Elsewhere, Totnes, Dartmouth, Kingsbridge and Ivybridge are relatively well provided but there are large numbers of parishes with little or no provision for the elderly which, in view of the numbers of retired persons living locally, must pose some cause for concern. In particular, parishes such as Aveton Gifford, Malborough, Modbury, Stokenham and Kingswear all had high proportions of their populations retired – over 25 per cent and, in cases, more than 30 per cent (at the 1971 census) – but had no local housing provision for the elderly.

The range of types of accommodation can also be described in terms of size (number of bedrooms), type of housing (bungalow, house or flat) and in dates of construction (as this will usually influence standards of physical construction and amenity provision). Various types of accommodation may well not suit certain applicants – for example, many families with children would not be very interested in flats other than those on the ground floor and with gardens, and many elderly people would prefer a bungalow to a house. Therefore, the proportion of housing available in the various types in different locations is of great relevance to its efficient and equitable allocation to tenants.

There is no simple distributional pattern of house types although a large proportion of parishes (twenty out of the sixty or so with council houses) have no bungalows at all but only houses or flats. In particular, some of the coastal areas have relatively few (if any) bungalows considering their generally more elderly populations. Chivelstone, East Portlemouth, Kingston, Bigbury, Kingswear, Dittisham, Holne and West Buckfastleigh have no bungalow accommodation and Slapton, Stokenham, Malborough and South Huish have very little (fewer than ten bungalows in each). By contrast, certain parishes have quite large numbers of bungalows. Around one-third or more of the local authority housing stock in Yealmpton, Holbeton, Strete, Sparkwell, Aveton Gifford, South Pool (78 per cent), Stoke Fleming (51 per cent) and Thurleston (50 per cent) is in the form of bungalows. In the main towns, proportions are much smaller: Totnes (bungalow accommodation, 9 per cent of total), Dartmouth (4 per cent), Kingsbridge (1 per cent) and Salcombe (4 per cent), although Ivybridge has 18 per cent of its local authority housing as bungalows.

Flats are also distrtibuted unevenly. Only Kingsbridge and Dartmouth have any large concentrations of flats, with 49 per cent of Darmouth's local authority accommodation being in flats of some type (ground, first, second or third floor). 17 per cent of Kingsbridge's accommodation is in the form of ground floor flats and 17 per cent in first and second floor flats. Only in Loddiswell and West Alvington (near Kingsbridge) are there any other relatively large proportions of these and here numbers are not great, as there are only ten ground floor and ten first floor flats or fewer in each. However, the large proportions of flats in Dartmouth and Kingsbridge do have significance for applicants to these two main parishes, especially as other accommodation may be very limited or under strong competition. They may, in fact, represent an important constraint upon the type and suitability of accommodation which applicants may be successful in obtaining in these parishes.

The age of housing is also an important consideration because older housing tends to be more poorly appointed than newer housing in terms of both physical condition and amenity provision. At a sub-district level, the four main SHDC housing districts of Totnes, Kingsbridge, Ivybridge and Dartmouth (Salcombe represents a fifth district but is effectively only composed of the two parishes of Salcombe and Malborough) do have very different proportions of their overall local authority housing stock in different ages of construction. Table 5.3 illustrates this quite convincingly. From this, it may be seen that Dartmouth and Ivybridge have the highest proportions of the oldest stock (although absolute numbers of pre-First World War dwellings are small). Almost one-quarter of Totnes's local authority stock was of pre-1945 construction and sizeable proportions of this older housing are also to be found in Dartmouth and Ivybridge. In all the districts, however, a great deal of the housing dates from the years 1946 to 1955. Almost one-half of Salcombe's housing and 42 per cent of Dartmouth's housing dates from this period.

Table 5.3
Housing districts : date of construction
of local authority housing

District	Pre- W.W.I.	Inter War	1946– 1955	1956– 1965	1966– 1975	1976– 1979	Total
Dartmouth	3.2	14.2	41.8	12.2	22.2	6.4	100.0
Ivybridge	3.8	18.7	34.9	9.2	15.1	18.3	100.0
Kingsbridge	0.1	12.8	35.7	16.2	16.8	18.4	100.0
Salcombe	1.5	6.7	49.2	11.8	28.7	2.1	100.0
Totnes	0.7	24.8	32.9	12.4	13.7	15.7	100.0
Total	1.7	17.6	36.4	12.6	17.0	14.7	100.0

The local authority housing surge immediately after 1974–1975 has reduced the relative importance of older housing in Ivybridge, Kingsbridge and Totnes Districts. In these areas, only about one-third of their local authority housing stock was built in the immediately postwar decade. Instead, Kingsbridge and Ivybridge each have over 18 per cent of their stock of recent construction and Totnes has 15 per cent. Viewed in another way, it can be stated that over ninety per cent of the post-1976 completions were in these three districts and, as was discussed earlier, Dartmouth fared quite badly in the wave of new building aimed at ending the large waiting list backlog and only 6 per cent of its stock is of post-1976 construction. This illustrates the effect of the protests which delayed the planned development of a new local authority estate in the

Dartmouth area and, as a result, well over one-half of its local authority housing stock dates to pre-1955, with the associated possibility that there may be physical and amenity deficiencies in much of the older housing.

The major locational feature of local authority housing in South Hams now seems to be its marked concentration into the four main settlements of Totnes, Kingsbridge, Dartmouth and Ivybridge. This is an important factor affecting the potential choices for applicants for housing and also those wishing to transfer between houses in SHDC. Approximate numbers of housing units (all types) in each of the main towns in 1979 are given below (Table 5.4).

Table 5.4
Housing in the main settlements (1979)

Parishes	No. of local authority dwellings
Ivybridge	300
Totnes (with	
Berry Pomeroy)	820
Kingsbridge	580
Dartmouth	680
Total	2,380

(Total SHDC housing stock = approximately 4,600 dwellings)

Therefore, some 51 per cent of all housing owned by SHDC is located in these four major settlements. If reference is made back to chapter four, it may be calculated that, in 1971, only 30.2 per cent of the population of the South Hams lived in these five towns (an estimated 1976 figure of 29.4 per cent). So, the four towns have a far greater concentration of local authority housing than would be justified purely on the basis of their population sizes. Outside these main towns, very few parishes have more than one hundred dwellings, the exceptions being Yealmpton (150 houses), South Brent (180 houses), Brixton (140 houses), and Modbury (100 houses), the numbers of houses being rounded for simplicity. This fact has a number of implications other than the obvious one that there will be very limited availability of local authority accommodation in other parishes. First, the SHDC has to make some form of allowance for persons who either require housing in parishes with small numbers of local authority houses or who are applying for housing from these parishes. There may be important reasons why people should require to live in some of the parishes with small local authority housing stocks, such as working in or near the parish or having relations there. Secondly, the parishes with small numbers of local authority houses may well be far more susceptible to pressure from tenants to buy their houses. In parishes with, for example, only ten or fewer local authority houses, these will not be on estates and may be in attractive rural settings with large gardens and pleasant sites. Such sales could add to the already considerable pressure on waiting and transfer lists in these areas.

The SHDC make allowances for people wanting accommodation in these parishes with small housing stocks by weighting their applications with a higher number of points. Critical cut-off sizes are used to determine the award of extra points, these being villages (frequently coterminous with parishes) with fewer than fifteen local authority houses, fewer than twenty-nine, fewer than forty-nine and fewer than seventy houses. People who live in, or need to reside in, villages below these cut-off levels are awarded extra points to assist their applications. There is, however, a very large number of parishes which are influenced by this differential pointing scheme, as illustrated in Figure 5.8. All but about one dozen parishes have fewer than seventy houses and thus carry extra weighting in the pointing system. The implications of these different pointing schemes are considered further in chapter seven when the locational requirements and needs of applicants are discussed.

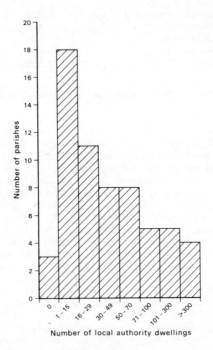

Figure 5.8: Parish distribution of local authority housing
Source: Appendix A

A final feature of the distribution of houses is that of house size, measured by number of bedrooms provided. This, too, tends to vary quite markedly across the SHDC area. The vast majority (98.7 per cent) of SHDC's housing stock is in the form of one-, two- and three-bedroom properties. Therefore, large families with three or more children have little chance of finding accommodation which will give each child a separate bedroom. The council owns only about fifty four-bedroom properties and almost all of these are concentrated in Dartmouth and Kingsbridge. The numbers of houses in other size categories are: one-bedroom, approximately 840 properties; two-bedroom, 1,200 and three-bedroom properties, approximately 2,500.

There are parishes in which certain sizes tend to predominate and this is important when, for example, there is a large proportion of one- and two-bedroom properties as these are usually inappropriate for family occupation. Two examples are that, in South Pool 21 out of 27 houses have one or two bedrooms, and in Ermington, 26 out of 36 houses have one or two bedrooms. A number of parishes, such as Yealmpton, Holbeton, Sparkwell and South Milton, have about one-third or more of their local authority housing stock in one-bedroom properties. The distribution of house sizes even in the main towns is not very evenly balanced and, as Table 5.5 shows, some of the towns have larger proportions of one type of accommodation than others; for example, Totnes has the largest proportion of two-bedroom properties and Dartmouth the most single bedroom properties.

Table 5.5
Bedroom numbers in local authority properties
in the main towns

(Percentages of total local
authority housing stock in each)

Town	Bedrooms				
	1	2	3	4+	Total
Ivybridge	24.7	17.2	57.5	0.0	100.0
Dartmouth	25.3	28.1	41.6	5.0	100.0
Totnes (incl. Berry Pomeroy)	12.5	30.4	56.4	0.7	100.0
Kingsbridge	24.9	20.4	52.8	1.7	100.0

Summary

In retrospect, this review of the housing stock in the South Hams, which focuses on the local authority sector in particular, illustrates a number of important features. The SHDC area shows higher than county averages of privately rented accommodation and lower proportions of local authority ownership. Certain parishes are completely without any local authority housing, although not as many parishes are totally devoid of local authority housing as has been seen in some other rural districts in England.

The housing stock overall has changed in recent years, increasing particularly in parishes around Plymouth and other main urban settlements, whilst recent local authority building has been concentrated in the main towns of Totnes, Ivybridge and Kingsbridge. The special feature of relatively large proportions of housing stock being held as second homes is of interest in parts of this picturesque district which is so popular for many forms of tourism and recreation. Whether this creates pressure on homes for locals is hard to determine although a case can certainly be argued that it causes higher local house prices than might otherwise be expected, especially in the smaller, country cottage types of property to which relatively lowly paid local inhabitants might look for purchase.

A review of the development of housing management since the creation of the South Hams District Council in 1974 would show that the local authority has developed a large and active Housing Department. This now has responsibility not only for the management of the local authority housing stock (and of overseeing sales to tenants where allowed and demanded), but it is also involved in the stimulation of a wide range of ventures involving public and private participation in housing. The existence of a body which should be able to take an overview and some concerted action with regard to housing is at least a step in the direction of the development of a coherent housing policy in this District which has problems of accessibility, and locational and structural imbalances in economic activity.

However, the housing stock over which the local authority has direct control has certain locational characteristics which are reflected in uneven distribution of types of houses, sizes and ages of construction. The concentration of a large proportion of housing into the main settlements is a particular feature and this inevitably biases the chances of applicants successfully obtaining, in a small parish, housing appropriate to their needs in locations near to their job and families. Such a concentration into the main settlements is an almost inevitable consequence of, or an adjunct to, the key settlement/selected local centre policies which concentrate service and employment provision into the major designated settlements. What these locational features mean in terms of the management of housing in the District now forms the theme of the remainder of this book.

SECTION C

HOUSING NEED AND MANAGEMENT
IN SOUTH DEVON

6 Housing need

GENERAL CONCEPTS OF NEED

Bradshaw (1972) has identified four major aspects of need: these are normative need (as defined by administrators), felt need (as expressed by individuals in interviews or questionnaire surveys), expressed need (involving an actual application or demand for particular services) and comparative need (ascertained by studying the characteristics of those actually in receipt of a service). Each of these concepts can be applied in the field of housing need and local authority provision. Those with a felt need for local authority housing may express this need in an application for rehousing, which will be evaluated by the housing managers in terms of normative need. The comparative needs of the applicants can be identified through studying their housing circumstances before and after rehousing.

The analysis in this and the following chapters concentrates on two of these concepts – namely expressed need, as can be identified in the waiting and transfer lists, and normative need, as revealed in the allocative methods of the local authority. Studies of social service provision (Pinch 1979, 1980) have shown that a distinction and possibly a conflict may exist between the expressed needs of the general public and the values of those who define normative need. These divisions also apply to housing need and policy. Not all those with felt needs will actually express them in applications for rehousing (perhaps because they perceive there to be an inadequate supply of dwellings available), even though some could be in need in normative terms. Conversely, many of those with expressed needs may not have normative needs; perhaps their own assessment of overcrowding does not match the official definition of this. Some of these themes will be investigated in the remainder of this book. This chapter begins by examining the expressed needs of those in the South Hams.

WAITING LISTS AND TRANSFER LISTS

In the local authority sector in the South Hams, the housing register (waiting list) and transfer list are the main indicators of expressed need. Through an analysis of these it is possible to identify the main social characteristics of the applicants and some features of their expressed needs. It should be noted that the assessment of both of these is influenced by the format of the official application forms which, being highly structured, allow the applicants only restricted opportunities to express their needs. Appendix A contains further details of the information contained in the waiting and transfer lists.

There are different application forms for those applying for
a first council house and for existing tenants wishing to be
rehoused by the local authority (see chapter seven). Although
there are some questions which are common to both, there are
also many which are different. For example, those applying
to the waiting list are asked about their employment status,
and transfer list applicants are asked whether they own a
car. Furthermore, those on the waiting list are asked to give
reasons in support both of rehousing and of their choice of
parish, while those on the transfer list are asked only to state
reasons in support of the former. As a result, a full systematic
comparison of the expressed needs of those on the two lists
is not possible. However, given the importance of evaluating
the provisions made for these two groups, wherever possible
an attempt will be made to compare their needs.

Another difference between the waiting lists and transfer
lists lies in the dates when these registers were compiled.
The transfer list is made up of applications lodged 'in recent
years' and, although Housing Department officials try to keep
this up-to-date by removing requests which are no longer active,
the list inevitably contains out-of-date information. In contrast,
the waiting list was completely revised in late 1979 as one
of the changes introduced by the new Chief Housing Officer
(see chapter seven). New application forms were sent out to
all those on the housing register so that all the information
contained in these was more or less current. At the time of
this research, there were 1000 applicants on the waiting list
and 531 on the transfer list. Further methodological information
regarding the transfer and waiting lists is provided in Appendix A.

It is possible to identify a number of features of the family
circumstances and present housing circumstances of those on
both lists. The age profiles of the applicants are broadly similar
and both lists include a substantial proportion of elderly persons
at, or approaching, retirement age (see Table 6.1). This is
a stage in the life cycle when both material and familial circumstances are changing (Rossi 1955), often necessitating a change
in housing. The only major difference between the applicants
is the higher proportion of those on the transfer list who are
in the middle age group. This difference can be seen more
sharply in the family sizes of the two groups. Almost three-
quarters of those on the waiting list are either single or have
only one other member in their family. In contrast, a little
more than half the transfer list applicants have three or more
members in their families. Therefore clear differences do emerge
between these groups. Those on the waiting list are more likely
to be the young or the elderly living alone or with one other
person, while those on the transfer list are more likely to
be middle aged and to have larger families. Both are likely
to feel housing needs associated with changes in the family
life cycle but they are at different stages within this.

Differences in the housing circumstances of the two groups
are of course to be expected as they live in different tenures.
Table 6.2 compares the types of dwelling that waiting and

transfer list applicants live in with the types of properties owned by the local authority. The comparison between the type of accommodation of those on the transfer list and the composition of the total stock of local authority housing is interesting. In relative terms those living in houses or bungalows are far less likely than those in flats or maisonettes to apply for transfers. This confirms the findings of other studies (Bird 1976; Taylor 1979) that flats are an unpopular type of accommodation. Although there are no high rise flats in South Hams, the lack of privacy or of a separate garden still seem to make two-storey flats unpopular. There seem to be fewer differences between waiting list and transfer list applicants: similar proportions live in houses, flats, and bungalows.

Table 6.1
Age and family size of applicants

Percentages

Age			Family size		
Age (years)	W.L.	T.L.	No. of persons in family	W.L.	T.L.
Less than 30	25.8	22.0	1-2	72.2	49.5
30 - 59	36.9	44.3	3-4	23.1	38.6
60 and over	35.6	33.7	5+	3.9	11.9
No information	1.7		No information	0.8	
Total	100.0	100.0	Total	100.0	100.0

W.L. = Waiting List
T.L. = Transfer List

Source: see Appendix A

Table 6.2
Type of accommodation

Dwelling type	Percentages		Local authority housing stock
	W.L.	T.L.	
Flats, maisonettes, and bedsitters	26.0	30.0	17.4
Bungalows	7.6	7.7	13.4
Houses	54.7	58.0	68.8
Others	7.8		0.4
No information	3.9	7.3	
Total	100.0	100.0	100.0

These similarities are of course superficial, as can be seen from a closer examination of housing circumstances. First, of those on the waiting list classified as living in 'other' types of accommodation, many are resident in caravans or hotels. Secondly, while all local authority tenants have some measure of security of tenure, this only applies to 48.6 per cent of those on the waiting list. Of the remainder, 20 per cent are sharing with friends or relatives, 5 per cent are in winter lets, and 17.9 per cent live in various other types of accommodation, including tied cottages. Therefore a substantial number of applicants do not live in a 'normal' regulated tenancy, although a surprisingly large group (presumably the elderly) do own their own homes. Thirdly, about one-fifth of all applicants from the privately-rented sector live in tied accommodation. Obviously not all of these are faced with imminent eviction, but their tenure arrangements represent a potential source of future acute housing need which could lead to substantial demands on the local authority for statutory rehousing (see chapter seven). Finally, while all existing local authority tenants would be expected to have the basic household amenities, large numbers of those on the waiting list lack or share the following – a kitchen (24 per cent), a living room (23 per cent), bath or shower (27 per cent), wc (25 per cent), mains water (5 per cent) and mains electricity (1 per cent). Therefore, beyond the superficial similarities in the types of accommodation in which waiting list and transfer list applicants live, the former clearly do experience far more acute housing need. They have less security of tenure and far poorer household amenities. Therefore a large number of applicants exist who, by almost any criteria, urgently require rehousing.

Finally, it is possible to identify some features of the socio-economic status of those with expressed housing needs. Amongst those on the waiting list only 56 per cent are economically active while most of the remainder are unemployed or retired. There are no comparable figures for transfer list applicants, but they do have a low level of car ownership (only 42 per cent). Another measure of wealth is provided by social class and with this it is possible to compare waiting list applicants with existing non transfer-listed applicants (a tenancy survey was carried out in 1980) and the South Hams population as a whole. Table 6.3 shows that on the whole, the least well off, the semi-skilled and unskilled manual, do figure disproportionately both as existing tenants and as applicants. Differences in the collection and coverage of these statistics make it impossible to draw more detailed inferences. However all the indicators, as would be expected, show that both waiting and transfer list applicants tend to be among the least well-off members of the community.

In summary, this brief review of the social characteristics of the applicants has identified two sources of housing need, one being related to the physical aspects of present housing circumstances and the other to adjustments associated with the family life-cycle. Neither of these represents anything like a homogeneous source of need for there are major differences between, and within, the groups of waiting list and transfer list applicants. This is most clearly revealed in the waiting list which contains applications both from owner occupiers and those living in short lease winter lets and caravans.

Table 6.3
Social class features of tenants and applicants

Percentages

	Waiting list applicants, 1980	Heads of households tenancy survey (8 per cent), 1981	Economically active in South Hams (census), 1971
Non-manual	25.3	9.4	41.5
Skilled-manual	36.6	43.7	30.4
Semi-skilled and unskilled manual	38.1	46.9	28.1
Total	100.0	100.0	100.0

Expressed reasons for rehousing

Thus far the analysis has concentrated on drawing inferences about housing need from the social and housing characteristics of the applicants. However, the application forms also allow for reasons to be stated in support of rehousing. These are un- structured but it is possible to classify them into 43 types of reasons, which are further aggregated into nine broad groups, shown below in Table 6.4. Most applicants stated only one or two reasons in support of their rehousing but some gave as many as five reasons. However, they have all been treated equally in this analysis irrespective of the number given and the listed order. These reasons are the best measure available of the felt need underlying the applications, and their analysis is therefore of particular importance.

Table 6.4
Grouped reasons given in support of rehousing

Percentages

Reasons	W.L.	T.L.
Health	14.1	13.7
Proximity of work/services	5.8	13.9
Family changes	21.0	6.6
Proximity to friends/relatives	3.4	7.0
Type of property/garden	23.7	22.3
Space requirements	6.5	15.9
Dislike of present area	3.1	9.5
Preference for other house/area	1.8	6.8
Other reasons	20.5	4.4
Total	100.0	100.0

Health reasons seem to be of equal importance in both groups. Otherwise, there are important differences between the waiting and transfer lists, and these will be outlined while at the same time some of the more important of the disaggregated 43 reasons will be identified.

Waiting list applicants most frequently cited family changes, type of property/garden and 'other' reasons in support of their rehousing; each of these was given as a reason by about a fifth of all applicants. Among family change reasons, a number of factors associated with starting a family were given such as 'marriage', 'childbirth', or 'pregnancy', 'desire to start own home' and 'desire to adopt or to start a family' (12.3 per cent of all reasons). Other family reasons were also given such as marital disputes or retirement but these were less important. This conforms with the impressions about housing need suggested by the earlier study of age and family size characteristics. The other two main groups or reasons are overlapping; the type of property reasons given are fairly broad ones such as 'general unsuitability' (8 per cent) and 'living in tied accommodation' (5.2 per cent), and the 'other' reasons include expired tenancies (11.5 per cent), eviction (2.3 per cent) and financial problems (5.9 per cent). Therefore, in addition to a group of applicants with specific stage of family life-cycle needs, there is also a second and larger group with immediate housing need arising from anticipated homelessness and/or the general unsuitability of their accommodation.

For transfer list applicants the most important reasons for rehousing are type of property/garden, followed by space requirements, proximity to work/services and health reasons. Unlike waiting list applicants, family changes are not widely given in support of rehousing. Indeed, the only major group of reasons commonly cited by both sets of applicants is 'type of property/garden'. Even here the similarity is superficial for, whereas waiting list applicants gave reasons of general unsuitability, transfer list applicants gave far more specific reasons such as 'desire for a garden' (4.8 per cent), 'desire for a ground floor flat' (4.3 per cent) and 'problems of upkeep of garden' (3.1 per cent). Proximity to work/services was also frequently given as a reason, particularly 'proximity to work' (6.7 per cent), 'nearness to schools, shops or personal social services' (4.0 per cent) and complaints about 'remoteness' or a desire for the 'convenience of centrality' (2.5 per cent). Additionally, transfer list applicants were twice as likely as waiting list applicants to give proximity to friends or relatives (7.0 per cent) as a reason. Locational considerations therefore are far more important reasons for rehousing for existing council tenants than for those on the housing register.

The other major group of reasons given by existing tenants, and again one that waiting list applicants were far less likely to cite, is 'space requirements'. A detailed breakdown of this shows a fairly even division between those requiring 'more bedrooms' or considering themselves to be 'overcrowded' (8.2 per cent) and those who consider themselves to be 'under-occupied'

(7.7 per cent). Obviously the latter reason is unlikely to be given by a waiting list applicant, but it does reveal why some housing authorities give preference to rehousing those from the transfer list (see chapter three). In a number of cases there exist families who consider themselves to be under-occupying large houses: if these families can be rehoused it will free a larger house for allocation. Finally, with respect to the differences between the two sets of applicants, it can be observed that existing tenants are three times more likely to give as reasons for rehousing the 'dislike of present area' or a 'preference for other house/area'; the most important single reasons within this group are 'neighbour problems' and 'attachment to a particular property'.

In summary, it has been observed that the expressions of housing need by those on the waiting and transfer lists are quite dissimilar, in that fundamentally different types of reasons are given by each group. Whereas the waiting list applicants tend to be those starting a family or those with immediate housing problems such as imminent homelessness, existing tenants are seeking rehousing so as to obtain more, or less, room, improved access to work, services, friends and relatives, more or less, garden space, and a more desirable house or area. This group of reasons clearly represents a form of 'finer tuning' of housing to meet current needs and aspirations.

Another aspect of the expression of housing need can be seen in the preference stated for a particular type of dwelling. Waiting list forms do not include this question but transfer list applications include questions concerning both the preferred type of accommodation and the preferred number of bedrooms. A sharper focus can be given to both analyses by comparing these preferences to the present type of accommodation and numbers of bedrooms being occupied. This should reveal whether there are any major movements out of, into or between types of properties.

The earlier analysis of the present housing circumstances of applicants had shown that those who lived in flats were more likely to be on the transfer list than those who lived in houses and bungalows. It is therefore to be expected that this would be reflected in a comparison of present and preferred accommodation type, as indeed it is (see Table 6.5). First, it is observed that houses are overwhelmingly the preferred accommodation type, with 61.2 per cent giving this as their first choice. Bungalows are the second most popular choice with flats bringing up the rear as the least preferred option. Disaggregation of these figures is interesting. More than two-thirds of those living in houses or bungalows would prefer to be rehoused in the same type of accommodation, but only 27.6 per cent of those living in flats would prefer another flat (and most of these prefer ground floor flats). The unpopu-larity of flats which was earlier inferred is therefore substantiated.

The earlier analysis also showed that there were significant numbers of transfer list applicants who considered themselves to be underoccupied or overcrowded/lacking bedrooms. More insight on this is available from a comparison of present and preferred numbers of bedrooms (see Table 6.6). The major feature of this table is to show that the main expressed need is for larger dwellings, with more than half the applicants preferring three or four bedrooms. The small number actually opting for four bedrooms may be due to a general awareness that only a small number of these are available. If the relationship between present, and preferred, numbers of bedrooms is examined, then it can be seen that the predominant preference is for transfer from smaller to larger homes. Those with one bedroom would prefer one or two bedrooms, those with two bedrooms would prefer two or three bedrooms, while those with three bedrooms would prefer the same number.

Table 6.5
Present and preferred type of accommodation
of transfer list applicants

Percentages

Preferred type

Present type	House	Flat	Bungalow	Total
House	69.7	9.5	20.6	100.0
Flat	55.2	27.6	17.2	100.0
Bungalow	13.5	13.5	73.0	100.0
Total	61.2	14.9	24.0	100.0

Table 6.6
Present and preferred number of bedrooms
of transfer list applicants

Percentages

Preferred number

Present number	1	2	3	4	Total
1	42.0	45.5	12.3		100.0
2	19.2	41.5	39.3		100.0
3	12.0	30.7	53.6	3.7	100.0
Total	19.5	36.3	41.9	2.3	100.0

However, although most applicants want more, or at least the same number, of bedrooms, there are a significant number who would prefer fewer bedrooms. Almost a fifth of those with two bedrooms want only one bedroom and, even more strikingly, of those with three bedrooms, 30.7 per cent want one fewer bedroom and 12.0 per cent want two fewer bedrooms. Therefore, a larger number of applicants than is suggested by the expressed reasons for transfers would prefer fewer bedrooms. This again highlights the importance of efficient transfer policies which can efficiently utilise the available housing resources.

The analysis of the transfer and waiting lists thus far has indicated a number of features of housing need seen through the social characteristics of the applicants, their reasons for being rehoused and their preference for other types of dwellings. One theme which has only briefly been mentioned so far but which underlies these patterns of need is the locational consideration, and this is examined in the following section.

LOCATION AND HOUSING NEED

The location of a house partly determines the proximity to friends, relatives, jobs, shops and services. Allocation of council houses therefore involves the allocation of varying levels of proximity. This is clearly important in urban areas where estates exist with poor access to jobs or shops, but it is particularly important in rural areas where greater distances and poorer public transport facilities will exaggerate these problems (see chapter two). Furthermore, the nature of rural local authority housing, with only small clusters of council houses outside the larger settlements, will limit the opportunities for rehousing in particular types of accommodation in particular areas as suggested in chapter five. It is therefore of considerable importance in assessing rural housing need that the locational aspects are understood.

The first feature to note is the distribution of the applicants. There are of course differences between the transfer list and the waiting list as the former, by definition, is restricted to people living in SHDC. In contrast, a surprisingly large proportion of waiting list applicants (16.3 per cent) are resident outside South Hams. This may be an indicator of the popularity of the area and of the pressures on housing locally. Leaving aside the applicants from outside the area, it is possible to compare the distribution of those on the waiting and transfer lists (see Figures 6.1 and 6.2).

There are similarities between the maps. The largest numbers of applicants in both cases are resident in the four largest settlements, namely Totnes, Kingsbridge, Dartmouth and Ivybridge. For transfer requests, the next most important areas are Salcombe, Brixton, Yealmpton and South Brent. As these eight areas have the largest numbers of local authority houses, it is not surprising that they should also have the largest numbers of transfer requests. In both lists, then, there is a high level of concentration of housing need. Some 57 per cent of transfer applicants and 39 per cent of waiting list applicants are from the four main settlements alone. Outside of these centres there is an extensive rural area where the absolute numbers of applicants are very small. In the high status parish of Woodleigh there are no transfer list applicants (since there are no council houses) or waiting list applicants. Even allowing for such

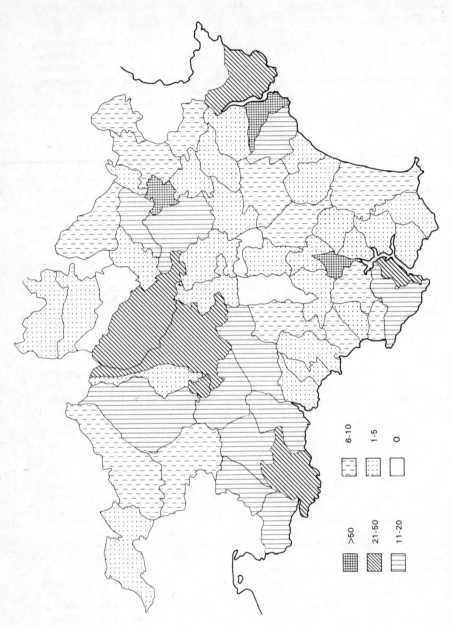

Figure 6.1: Residential distribution of waiting list applicants from within South Hams 1980
Source: Appendix A

>50		6-10
21-50		1-5
11-20		0

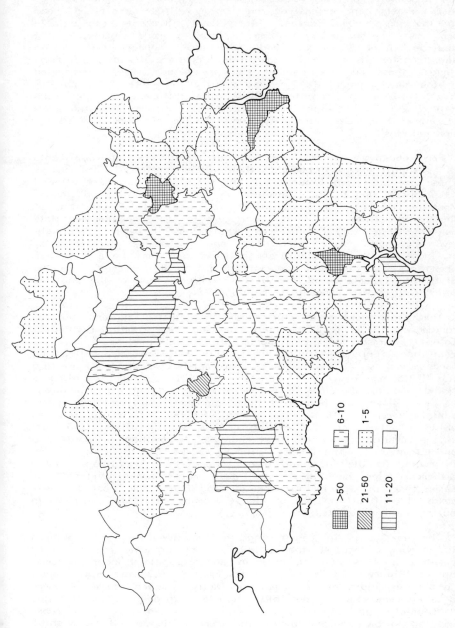

Figure 6.2: Residential distribution of transfer list applicants 1980
Source: Appendix A

>50

21-50

11-20

6-10

1-5

0

extreme examples, the majority of parishes have fewer than ten applicants on each list. Therefore, outside the major centres there exists an extensive 'rump' of diffuse expressed need in the more rural areas. This clearly presents considerable problems for housing management. Looking more closely at the distribution of those in need, differences between the waiting and transfer lists can be identified. As has already been mentioned, those on the transfer list are rather more concentrated in the major centres (as also is the housing stock - see chapter five). Waiting list applicants are more diffuse and fewer than half live in the eight most important parishes. In this case therefore there are potentially even greater problems for allocation policies.

For housing policies the present residences of applicants is probably less important than their preferred residences. These are shown in Figures 6.3 and 6.4. Applicants are allowed to express up to four preferences on the application forms. Most express at least one preference, and only 8 per cent of those on waiting lists and 4 per cent of those on transfer lists do not state any preferences whatsoever. However, relatively few applicants state more than one preference: for example, of those on the transfer list, only 40 per cent have a second preference, 18 per cent have a third and 8 per cent a fourth. Given the importance of the first preference, most of the analysis which follows will concentrate on this.

The preferences show the same concentrated pattern as the residences. The most important parishes are again Ivybridge, Totnes, Kingsbridge and Dartmouth, with parishes such as Yealmpton, Brixton, South Brent and Salcombe also attracting large numbers of applicants. Approximately two-thirds of waiting list (62.5 per cent) and transfer list (63.1 per cent) applicants listed one of the four main settlements as their first choices. As a corollary of this, most other parishes had very few applicants. There were 16 parishes which were not the first preferences of either those on the waiting or the transfer lists, and most of the remainder were the first choice of fewer than ten applicants on either list. The policy dilemma posed by this distribution is acute. On the one hand there does exist a significant diffuse preference for housing in the more rural areas, yet at the same time the small numbers of applicants for most parishes make it difficult to obtain the economies of scale inherent in building larger estates.

The next step in considering the locational features of need is to bring together the distribution of present and preferred residences. This can be done in an aggregate manner by comparing Figures 6.1 and 6.2 with Figures 6.3 and 6.4. Visual comparison indicates a broad similarity between these. A more detailed analysis is possible, however, through examining the individual applications: these can be sub-divided into those wishing to be rehoused within the same parish and those wishing to be rehoused in another parish. Table 6.7 summarises the proportions preferring to be rehoused in the same parish, for waiting and transfer lists and for the four main settlements

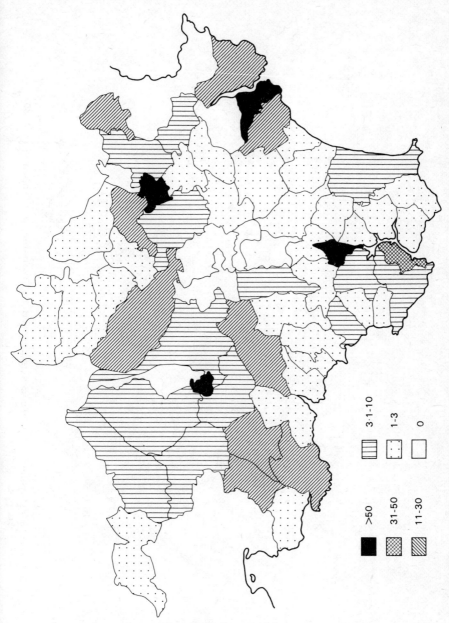

Figure 6.3: First parish preferences expressed by waiting list applicants 1980
Source: Appendix A

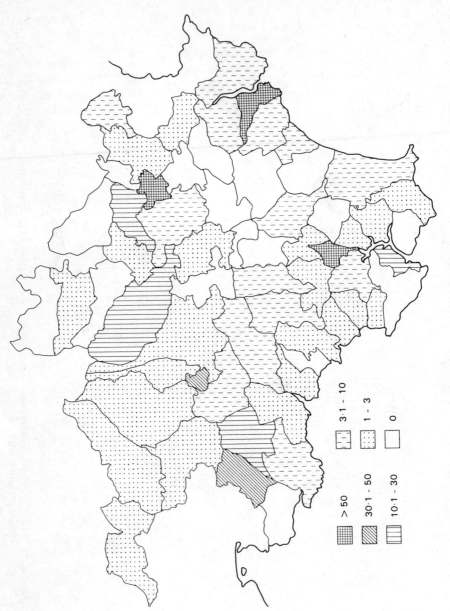

Figure 6.4: First parish preferences expressed by transfer list applicants 1980

Source: Appendix A

> 50

30·1 - 50

10·1 - 30

3·1 - 10

1 - 3

0

separately.

Table 6.7
Preference for rehousing in the
parish of present residence

| Settlements | Percentage who prefer parish of residence | |
	W.L.	T.L.
Four major settlements	80.2	73.0
Other 'more rural' parishes	38.0	48.6
Total	55.4	64.4

There are important differences evident in this table. In general, the majority of applicants prefer to be rehoused in the same parish, although this is more likely for those on the transfer lists than those on the waiting lists. There is, however, a major difference between those living in the larger settlements and those living in the more rural parishes. More than 70 per cent of those on both the waiting and the transfer lists living in Ivybridge, Dartmouth, Kingsbridge or Totnes preferred to be rehoused in the same parish. Fewer than half of these living in the more rural areas wanted to remain in the same area. There is, therefore, a significant number of applicants who consider that their housing need can be partly ameliorated through moving to another parish.

The next stage is to identify the actual pattern of preferred inter-parish rehousing. The main preferred inter-parish moves are shown in Figures 6.5 and 6.6. There are similarities between these two maps in that, generally, most of the preferred inter-parish moves are over fairly short distances and are from more rural parishes into the adjacent major settlements. Essentially, therefore, a pattern of concentration exists in these preferred moves. However, this simple pattern must be modified in two ways. First, there are important preferred flows between more rural areas, especially in the south-west between Yealmpton, Brixton and Newton and Noss (these maps tend to underemphasise these rural-rural moves as there are a very large number of single person flows which have had to be omitted). Secondly, not all the major settlements seem to be equally popular. The two which are more accessible, Totnes and Ivybridge, attract relatively large numbers of applicants from both the waiting and transfer lists. Kingsbridge, however, although attracting a very large number of waiting list applicants seems relatively unpopular with existing tenants. Most of the inter-parish transfer requests involving Kingsbridge are outflows; these are of two types, either to attractive locations in Stokenham and Salcombe or to other towns, particularly the more accessible Totnes. Dartmouth seems to be even more unpopular with existing tenants,

101

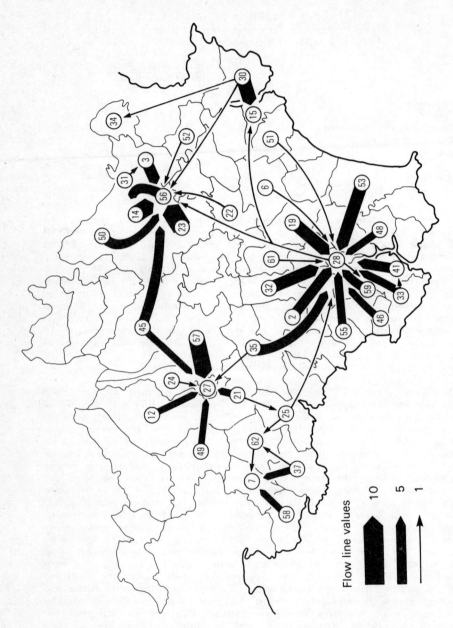

Flow line values

10

5

1

Figure 6.5: Major inter-parish applications: first expressed preferences
(waiting list 1980)
Source: Appendix A

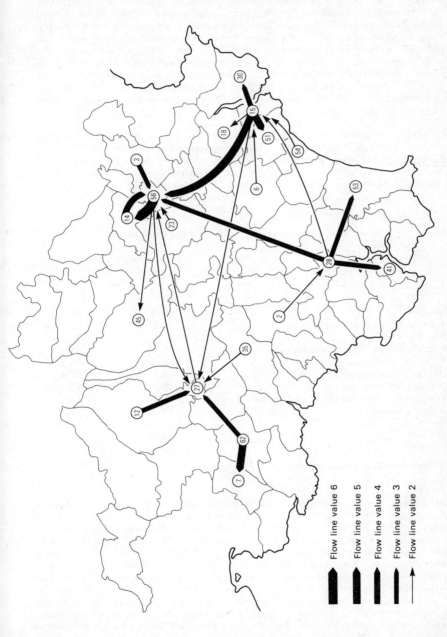

Flow line value 6

Flow line value 5

Flow line value 4

Flow line value 3

Flow line value 2

Figure 6.6: Major inter-parish applications: first expressed preferences
(transfer list 1980)
Source: Appendix A

having substantial preferred outflows both to adjacent parishes and to Totnes. In summary, these spatial patterns indicate a crude hierarchy of settlements. Totnes acts as something of a 'regional' centre attracting applicants from most parts of the SHDC except the west. Otherwise most moves are fairly localised with Totnes, Ivybridge and Kingsbridge (less so for transfers) exercising a strong influence in their 'sub regions'. Finally there is a lower tier of rural parishes which mainly provide preferred out-movement. Dartmouth would seem to fit into this latter category but its unpopularity should not be exaggerated, for most applicants from Dartmouth would prefer to remain in the town.

Finally, another locational aspect of housing need can be studied through examining the relationships between parish preference and the expressed reasons for rehousing. Table 6.8 shows the percentage who wish to remain in the same parish for each of the main groups of reasons for rehousing.

Table 6.8
Reasons for rehousing and parish preference

| | Percentage who wish to remain in same parish | |
Reasons	T.L.	W.L.
Health	45.9	67.2
Proximity to work/services	22.6	29.9
Family changes	63.1	70.3
Proximity to friends/relatives	*	30.3
Type of property/garden	60.0	65.8
Space requirements	69.6	71.6
Dislike of present area	*	57.8
Preference for other area/house	*	68.2
Other reasons	53.5	76.2
Total	55.4	66.4

* Percentages not calculated if numbers smaller than 30

A clear and consistent pattern is observed in this table. The lowest proportions of those wanting to stay in the same parish are persons expressing proximity to work/services or to friends/relatives as reasons in support of their applications. Fewer than 50 per cent of those on the transfer list giving health reasons for rehousing also wish to remain in the same parish. This is as should be expected: the pattern of preferred rural-urban or urban-urban mobility that was observed earlier is a function of the desire for improved accessibility to friends, relatives, shops, services, jobs and perhaps, health services. Those with other reasons for being rehoused are likely to prefer to stay in the same area. This is particularly true of those who require rehousing because of changes in their family circumstances in order to obtain more/less amounts of space. Therefore, there is evidence of very strong attachment to local areas, unless a move is essential, as it presumably is, to improve accessibility.

The overall picture which has emerged from this analysis of need is by no means a simple one. The expressed housing needs of those on the waiting and transfer lists are quite different, and considerable variety also exists within these major groups. Those with expressed needs range from elderly owner-occupiers unable to maintain their homes to young married couples with children who perhaps are sharing a house with relatives or living in a short lease winter let. In between, there are a number of other categories of those in need, including transfer requests for larger or smaller properties, those requiring improved accessibility and those who like/dislike particular areas or houses. The housing managers faced with this array of needs have only a single (if heterogeneous) supply of housing available, and in practice have only a small number of vacant relettings and an even smaller number of new dwellings available. Their problems are compounded in two ways. First, there seems to be a preference for houses and bungalows so that these dwellings are probably oversubscribed compared to flats. Secondly, the locational aspects of need further restrict the options that are available. There is a high level of preference for rehousing in the same parish, which can be a source of considerable difficulties in the more rural parishes with very small numbers of dwellings. Also some towns are clearly more popular than others, so that the demand for rehousing is spatially uneven. Therefore, there has to be some method of reconciling competing demands and claims and the following chapter examines the administrative methods which have been adopted by the SHDC to assess and to respond to this housing need.

7 Housing allocation policies

HOUSING MANAGEMENT IN THE SOUTH HAMS

Local authority housing management clearly involves far more than the simple allocation of applicants to suitable dwellings. Indeed the concept of what constitutes the role of a housing department has changed considerably in recent years, being broadened to include an assessment of overall housing need as well as a variety of policy measures ranging through housing associations and promoting private developments to administering improvement schemes. An illustration of this broader role can be seen from examining the contents of the HIPS submissions of the District Councils (see chapter three).

These developments have also occurred in the SHDC where the role of the housing department has changed out of all recognition in recent years. Prior to local government reform in 1974, there were seven different housing authorities in the South Hams, although not all were represented by separate housing departments: most were incorporated into other sections such as the Treasurer's or Technical Services Departments. As seen earlier in chapter five, there were considerable differences amongst the local authorities with regard to the level of public housing construction, and this is still evident today in the variations in provisions within the SHDC. The most striking example of this is the high level of elderly persons' accommodation in the western area, which is very much an inheritance from the very active lead taken in this field by the old Plympton Rural District.

The seven local authorities also had different housing allocation policies (which were then almost the only function of the housing administrators). Some of the authorities, but not all, had housing registers and these were based on varied and not always clearly defined criteria. The actual powers of allocation, more often than not, rested with the elected members rather than with the council officials. With local government reform imminent in 1974, a steering group was formed from officers representing the different authorities and they produced a simple points scheme, emphasising insanitary or overcrowded conditions. This was used to allocate points to everyone on the waiting list in the SHDC, so that from 1974 a single housing register and points scheme existed for the entire area. There was also a change in the control of allocations with agreement being reached that power should rest jointly between the members and the officials. As yet, however, housing was not a separate department and there were only four officials responsible for housing allocations.

The first points scheme was clearly oversimplistic and therefore in 1976 a more detailed scheme was introduced. However, the implementation of this scheme coincided with the completion of large numbers of new houses in the main settlements in 1977, as seen in chapter five. Still with only a minimal staff, the housing officers were barely able to keep up with the increased volume of work. Allocations became almost the sole function of the authority, if only because there was no time to develop other roles. There was still no housing department, responsibility for this resting successively in the Secretary's Department and the Chief Executive's Department in 1977-78 and 1978-79. All this was fundamentally changed in 1979 when it was decided to establish a separate Housing Department and appoint a Chief Housing Officer. This was accomplished with an outsider, with experience in a large urban authority in the South East, being appointed to run the Department. Under his guidance, housing, once a 'cinderella' function of the Council, has become one of the five major Departments and now has a total staff of twenty-one including five persons with housing management qualifications. Control over allocations has again changed with the Chief Housing Officer now being delegated powers to make all the allocations. The role of the Department has also been broadened and it is now actively engaged in promoting private development (notably in Kingsbridge where agreement has been reached that, in return for suitable land, the developers should sell the first 60 houses in a large estate to nominees of the council) and also in encouraging the activities of housing associations. Therefore, within seven years of local government reform, the housing functions of the SHDC have been transformed so completely that they would probably be unrecognisable to those who had known the older system.

However, despite adopting broader roles, the major function of the Department, insofar as it directly affects the lives of the residents of South Hams, remains the allocation of council houses. This is particularly true of the period early in 1980 when the research for this book was undertaken, for then most of these other schemes were still in embryo. Therefore, although it may not do full justice to the Housing Department to concentrate on allocations, these do represent the major resource at its disposal for responding to housing need.

Allocation is not a single, simple procedure, as the discussion in chapter three showed. Rather, there are a number of procedures involved which can be subdivided into six major stages, which an applicant for housing will usually go through sequentially:

1. The restrictions on the housing register and transfer list.
2. The methods for assessing need.
3. The criteria for the points scheme.
4. The types of queues formed.
5. The priorities in rehousing.
6. The actual allocation of particular properties to particular applicants.

These stages (which are discussed in general terms in chapter three) will be used to structure the examination of allocation methods in SHDC.

ENTRY TO LOCAL AUTHORITY HOUSING

Qualifications for entry

There are different entry qualifications for the transfer and waiting lists and there have also been recent changes in both of these, so therefore they will be considered separately.

Until late in 1979 acceptance onto the housing register was fairly restricted. Applicants either had to have three years' continuous residence or continuous employment in South Hams; otherwise they previously had to have been resident in the area for at least five years. These were very substantial restrictions which clearly must have made movement into the South Hams difficult for those requiring council houses. It can be imagined that this could have caused particular hardship for those working in the South Hams but living elsewhere, who would have faced three years of possibly lengthy commuting until they even qualified for a place on the Housing Register. There was also one further restriction in that applications could only be accepted from single applicants if they were over the age of 24. This again could be a source of stress either in preventing young adults from leaving a difficult family arrangement or in restricting their ability to move nearer jobs which might be located elsewhere in the South Hams. Given the centralised nature of employment in the area, which was outlined in chapter four, and the pattern of preferred rural-urban mobility seen in the previous chapter, this probably would have been a special problem in the smaller and more isolated villages.

Since April 1980, apparently through the common assent of both councillors and officials, these restrictions have been eased considerably, so that the SHDC now operates a fairly open register. Persons over the age of 18 living or working in the South Hams will be eligible to come onto the register, although they will only be allocated points after six months. In effect, then, a three-year qualification period has been reduced to six months. The reasons given for retaining this residential qualification are so as to be seen 'to be fair to locals', and also so as to correspond with the 1976 Homeless Persons Act, under which such a person becomes the responsibility of the local housing authority after six months' residence. Exceptions to this qualifying period may be made for key workers, the elderly with a family connection, social or medical need, or a lack of other satisfactory arrangements), those with five years' residence in the area within the last 20 years, members of the armed forces with strong local connections and those in tied agricultural accommodation (with at least two years in this employment). These exceptions do provide some scope for the relief of individual cases of hardship. Nevertheless, although the shorter qualification period is to be welcomed, it must still act as a barrier to the remedy of occasional cases of acute need amongst new residents or employees in the area.

The operation of the transfer list is far simpler, being open to all tenants in principle, although those with a poor rent paying record will not actually be considered for rehousing unless they show improvement over a three-month period. The one restriction is that after a transfer an applicant does not become eligible again for another transfer within twelve months. An exchange list is also operated which is open to all tenants; to improve the efficiency of this service it is now being developed into a board display in the Housing Department rather than a written list which tenants have to ask for to consult. Finally, since April 1981 the SHDC along with the other housing authorities in Britain has entered into the National Mobility Scheme, under which it agrees to make available 1 per cent of its lettings each year. In SHDC this is considered to represent two lettings each year and, as a mark of the popularity of the area, by June 1981 two applications had already been received and accepted under this scheme.

In recent years, then, the SHDC has moved towards far more open conditions of acceptance for rehousing. Nevertheless some restrictions remain, notably for recently-arrived residents or employees and, in common with all other housing authorities, for transfers between districts.

Assessing need

There are two stages in assessing need, the first depending on the type of method used, and the second upon the detailed criteria of the points systems used.

The SHDC housing authority has used a number of methods of differing degrees of formality. Before 1974 a number of the authorities did not have a formal points system for the housing register. Instead, the housing need of applicants was decided 'on merit' by the councillors. Since 1974, however, a more formal points system has been operated although, even with this, scope remains for some flexibility in assessing the points to be given. In contrast, the transfer list is still operated on an informal basis. Assessments of needs are made by the housing officials through their non-quantitative evaluation of the transfer application forms and the home visit reports. At the time of writing, however, the council was preparing a formal points scheme which was to be broadly similar to that operated for the waiting list.

The points scheme The most critical stage in assessing the needs of those on the housing register is the points scheme. This has changed in recent years, as has the information required from the applicants. Until late 1979 applicants were allocated points as follows in Table 7.1.

Table 7.1
The pre–1980 points scheme for the housing register

1. Overcrowding
Separate bedrooms are required for

   (a) husband and wife
   (b) one or two children of either sex below the age of 10
   (c) one or two children of the same sex 10 years of age or over

   For each additional bedroom required four points are given

2. Lack of separate home
Four points are given for sharing a kitchen, two points for sharing a bathroom/wc and four points for sharing a living room (up to a maximum of 10 points)

3. Sub–standard property
Based on a report from Technical Services Department, a maximum of 10 points can be awarded for this

4. Medical points
The community physician can award up to 10 points for medical need

5. Separated families
Five points can be given if wife, husband or children are forced to live apart through a lack of suitable accommodation

6. Discretionary points
The Housing Committee can award up to six points for this

7. Residence or work in area
Half a point can be given for each five years of residence or work in the area if the total of points of the applicants are otherwise equal

This scheme was clearly fairly crude, covering only a limited number of aspects of housing need. The special problems of rural accessibility, which were discussed earlier in chapter two, were barely acknowledged in this points scheme. It also incorporated substantial elements of discretionary pointing in at least three of the six main headings, which could be sources of potential conflict or confusion for the applicant. The new points scheme introduced in March 1980 goes some way towards rectifying both these features. Points are allocated under eleven different headings as outlined below in Table 7.2.

Table 7.2
Points scheme for the housing register 1980

Criteria   Points

1. Bed space deficiency

   Assuming that a separate bedroom is required
   for each of the following:

   i   Man and wife, lone parent, single and
        adult person

   ii   Each child except that
        a two children of same sex;
        b two children of opposite sex under
           seven years be permitted to share a
           double bedroom

   iii A person who, in the opinion of the
        Council's medical advisor, should sleep
        in a separate bedroom

   For each bed space deficient   5

   iv   Where a child, of necessity, must share
        a bedroom with a person of the same
        sex, but where there is a considerable
        age difference   3 - 5

2. Lack of, or shared, facilities

		Family	Single
a	Lack of living room	8	3
	Share living room	4	2
b	Lack of kitchen	8	3
	Share kitchen	4	2
c	Lack of WC	8	3
	Share WC	4	2
d	Lack of bath/shower room	8	3
	Share bath/shower room	4	2

3. Lack of, or inadequate, services

a	Cold water	up to 5
b	Hot water	up to 2
c	Electricity	up to 3

Table 7.2 (contd.)

4. Lack of amenities

   Points to be awarded according to the particular circumstances of the applicant reflecting
   the following:

   i   Play space for children

   ii Clothes drying facilities and garden size

   iii Storage space

   iv Isolation and access to property   Maximum 6

5. Separated families

   Points awarded to families who have been
   separated for at least six months for no other
   reason than that they have no accommodation
   in which they can live together   10

6. Environmental health deficiencies

   Awarded to take account of unfit and sub-
   standard accommodation factors not reflected
   elsewhere in the points scheme   up to 5

7. Medical points

   To be awarded by the Council's medical advisor
   after consideration of medical evidence   up to 20

8. Length of time in need on Housing Register

   Where an applicant's points total has reached
   within 10 points below the current rehousing
   level in their particular bedroom allocation
   category and area of choice, for each period
   of at least twelve months thereafter, 2 points
   to be awarded annually in April of each year   2 – 10

9. Length of residence in area

   1 point to be awarded for each five years the
   applicant has resided within the district   1 – 5

10. Discretionary points

    Points will be awarded where, in the opinion
    of the Chief Housing Officer, there are circum-
    stances causing some form of housing depriva-
    tion which is not covered within the points
    scheme   10

11. Village location points

    When considering allocations of property in
    particular villages, additional points will be
    awarded to applicants who reside, or need to
    reside, in that village   2 – 6

This new scheme represents an improvement over the previous scheme in a number of ways. First, more subtle pointing is available for those features which were also included in the earlier scheme. With regards to overcrowding (or bed space deficiency as it is now termed), allowance is made for those who need separate bedrooms on medical grounds, the age for separate bedrooms for children of different sex is lowered to seven, and points are also allocated where two children of the same sex but of considerably different ages have to share. The points for 'lack of separate facilities' (previously termed 'lack of separate home') have now been broadened under a category which includes shared main living rooms, kitchen and bathroom; the needs of families and single applicants are also distinguished under the new scheme. Discretionary points, separated family points, sub-standard property points and medical points are retained more or less unchanged although a proportionately larger number of points is awarded for the last named.

The second improvement is that some completely new features have been incorporated into the scheme. Points are now awarded if applicants lack or have inadequate services or if they lack amenities such as play space, clothes drying facilities or, interestingly, suffer from isolation or poor access to the property. Points are also to be awarded directly both for length of residence in the area and for length of time in need on the housing register. This reintroduces an element of residential qualification (not extended to those only working in the area) but, at the same time, probably correctly, acknowledges that those in 'moderate' need over a long period of time should be given greater recognition. Finally, village location points are awarded to those who reside in certain villages and this will be discussed later in this chapter.

Evaluating the points scheme In evaluating the points scheme, five main observations should be made. First, an objective scheme such as this necessarily treats all points equally, although two families with, say, the maximum number of points for sub-standard properties may actually live in quite different types of unfit properties; or, to take another example, two families may both have five points each for a deficient bedspace. However, whereas in one family the points are scored because a brother and sister aged 5 and 8 share a room, in the other family it may be because an adult son shares a room with his parents. Clearly, different types and levels of stress are associated with each of these arrangements although they both score equal numbers of points. This is a case where a mismatch exists between felt and normative need. There is no easy solution to the problem. Either a far more detailed points scheme is required in which case it becomes complex to administer and unintelligible to the applicant, or a more 'flexible' points scheme is required with the officials having greater discretionary powers. The housing officials themselves dislike this idea for they prefer the scheme to be simple to operate so that applicants can easily understand how their points are allocated. In general then, there does not seem to be any alternative conventional scheme available which could substantially improve on the simple points scheme used in SHDC.

Secondly, any points scheme provides a normative measure of need which may differ from expressed need which, in turn, may differ from felt need. For example, if an analysis is made of the bed space requirements of those who give 'overcrowding' or 'need more bedrooms' as expressed needs for rehousing, then it is seen that not all are in normative need. Given that the information recorded is accurate, then only 40 per cent of transfer list applicants and 52 per cent of the housing register applicants would officially be considered as needing more bed-rooms. If the expressed need is related to a strong feeling of overcrowding, then this could be a source of grievance for applicants. Further comment on this is not possible without additional behavioural research, but in any housing authority where there is a real and consistent difference between expressed and normative need, a re-evaluation of management policies would clearly be required.

The third reservation is connected with the points allocated to different types of need. Any normative evaluation of need, no matter how closely it tries to be sympathetic to felt or ex-pressed needs, will necessarily be arbitrary. For example, how are the needs of a separated family (ten points) to be equated with those of a family living together in a house without hot and cold water and electricity (which also scores ten points)? All that can be said in this respect with regard to the SHDC scheme is that there do not seem to be any glaring injustices in the points for different types of need. Whether or not there are felt to be injustices, only the applicants themselves know. The only aspect which seems contentious to the authors is the inclusion of points for length of residence. A family with five years' residence in the area is given five points which equals the number of points awarded to a family who are deficient of one bed space or to a family who lack a cold water supply. This does not seem to be an egalitarian equation even though it is possible to understand the local pressures which lie behind the points awarded for length of residence.

A fourth qualification is that up to ten discretionary points can be allocated by the Chief Housing Officer, which could be the equivalent of the points earned by a family lacking two bed spaces. The housing officials themselves are aware of this and would prefer a totally non-discretionary scheme. However, they point out that, naturally, no single points scheme could cater for unforeseen circumstances, and hence this discretionary element must be retained. It is used rarely and only when there are special conditions such as a family living in a shed. Unless therefore there is a sudden growth of shanty towns in the South Hams, this should not be a serious source of conflict!

A fifth reservation covers the types of need which are given normative recognition. The problems of overcrowding, substandard-ness and insecurity of tenure are all recognised in some way. These are the kinds of housing problems which would be expected in an area such as SHDC which experiences the twin pressures of agricultural and tourist development. However, another critical feature of housing need, accessibility, is neglected in the points scheme. Levels of accessibility to shops, jobs, services and relatives are important in rural areas generally (as seen in chapter two) and in South Hams, discussed in chapter four. Many transfer and some waiting list applicants have expressed housing needs relating to accessibility, yet there is no provision for this in the points system. Although it may be taken into account informally, it remains a notable omission from the formal assessment of need. Overall, in spite of the reservations which have been expressed, the points scheme used in SHDC seems fairly well balanced and sensitive to most aspects of housing need.

Every applicant also receives a home visit before points are allocated. Officially the purpose of this is to fill in missing data on the form and to verify that the information given is correct, although it also provides the opportunity to assess the cleanliness and condition of applicants' homes. The home visit report form contains a checklist of questions covering the marital status, medical circumstances, sleeping arrangements, and length of residence of the applicants, and also the rooms, services, facilities and amenities available to them.

The remainder of the points procedure in the SHDC is fairly simple and open. Each applicant is given a pamphlet which details how points are awarded and they are also told the number of points that they have been allocated. Applicants can check this total against the guidelines for the scheme and can therefore carry out their own assessment. If they are dis-satisfied with the number of points awarded, then they can appeal to the Chief Housing Officer and, if still not satisfied, to the Appeals Sub-committee of the Housing Committee. In the first twelve months of the new scheme it is interesting that no appeals went as far as the elected members, even though more than a thousand applicants were either pointed or repointed. This would seem to be a tribute to a fairly simple and easily understandable scheme which offers relatively little scope for conflict or misinterpretation.

However, one final problem associated with the points scheme remains. Being informed of the points awarded does not in itself indicate the probability of being rehoused. To understand this, a person would have to know the points awarded to others and the points scored by those currently being rehoused. The SHDC do not publicise either of these facts and very few authori-ties do so. The housing authority's position on this issue is that they would like to be able to tell applicants how likely rehousing is but that they also do not want to raise false hopes. For example, an applicant could be told that rehousing was likely within twelve months, but then unforeseen circumstances could extend this to two or three years. A method to circumvent this would simply be to publish an aggregate table of the points given to all applicants, although clearly this could also produce false hopes about rehousing. One thing is clear, however, that until a way is found of giving applicants a better indication of their rehousing prospects, many will continue to suffer the stress caused by uncertainty.

Finally, the assessment of transfer applicants needs to be considered. Although not formally pointed, it is interesting to note the information that they are required to provide (see Table 7.3).

Table 7.3
Information provided on transfer application forms

1. Number of bedrooms

2. Number of living rooms

3. Length of residence at address

4. Present type of property

5. Persons resident with applicant

6. Four choices for transfers

7. Preferred type of property

8. Preferred number of bedrooms

9. Place of employment

10. Availability of transport

11. Reasons in support of application

This information is broadly comparable to that provided on the waiting list application form, although it obviously does not contain questions on tenure, household amenities or previous residence. Therefore it should be possible to move to a pointing scheme which allows some comparison with those on the housing register. At present the assessment of transfer applicants seems to rest on occupancy rates, access to employment and the ex-pressed needs for rehousing.

ALLOCATION METHODS

Whereas most aspects of assessing need are governed by formal and quantitative methods, allocation procedures are less well-defined. There are three stages in allocation: queuing, decisions on priorities for rehousing, and the placement of individuals in dwellings. As an applicant advances through these stages and approaches actual allocation, so the procedures involved become increasingly less well-defined.

Queuing   The first step in allocation is the simplest. All waiting list applicants are placed into queues according to the type of dwelling for which they are eligible. This is not necessarily the same as the preferred type of dwelling. There are five queues and these are for accommodation for the elderly, other single applicants, married couples, those with one child, and those with two or more children. In effect, these are queues according to the numbers of bedrooms for which applicants are considered (normatively) to be eligible. Each of these major queues is further subdivided into five parts according to which of the five housing areas (internal administrative divisions) for which applicants have expressed preferences: Ivybridge North, Ivybridge South, Dartmouth, Totnes and Kingsbridge. Therefore, some twenty-five different queues exist and the probability of rehousing depends on the length of a particular queue in relation to the number of vacancies which occur in suitable dwellings. There will clearly be different waiting periods for each of these queues. Position in the queue is determined by the number of points obtained but it is possible, of course, that the same number of points may place an applicant near the front of one queue but only in the middle of another. At the time of writing, the longest queue was probably for accommodation for the elderly while the shortest queue was for three-bedroom dwellings. Those on the transfer list are also formally queued, according to the number of bedrooms they require and their preferred parish. Therefore, as with waiting list applicants, they are subject to variable waiting periods.

Priorities   Even when a waiting list applicant reaches the front of a queue or a transfer list applicant is considered to be amongst those in greatest need, this does not necessarily mean that rehousing is imminent. Instead the likelihood of rehousing depends on the priorities of the housing authority, not only between the waiting and transfer list but also in relation to other groups, especially the homeless, agricultural workers, those whose homes are under compulsory purchase orders, key workers and those with medical reasons. Although no official policy exists to differentiate the claims of these groups, it is possible to identify some of the authority's priorities.

The highest priority has to be allocated to the first three groups. The council is under a statutory obligation to rehouse homeless persons who have lived in South Hams for more than six months, agricultural workers living in tied accommodation which is now required by the ex-employer for a key worker, and those whose homes are to be demolished under a compulsory purchase order (see chapter three). The last named may not be very numerous in a predominantly rural area such as SHDC, but both the former categories could be fairly substantial. Beyond these groups the priorities seem less clear, but probably the next most favoured category are the key workers towards whom a 'positive policy' has been adopted (HIPS statement 1979). Those with medical grounds are also given a high priority. In a policy statement on waiting list applications there is a commitment to give priority rehousing to those with the maximum twenty medical points irrespective of the other points awarded. The remainder of the waiting and transfer list applicants are then considered 'on their merit'; this is indicated by the points total for the former while priority within the transfer list is given to those who are under-occupied, overcrowded or need to move closer to their employment (HIPS statement 1979). Therefore,

117

those on the waiting or transfer lists without strong medical grounds could find themselves fairly low in the priority list for rehousing, despite the high number of points they may have been awarded. On occasion, however, these priorities can be overturned when the authority makes a pragmatic decision to rehouse existing tenants so as to create a vacancy in a particular type of house or location which is in great demand.

Placement decisions Finally, when an applicant does reach the stage when there is priority for rehousing, he/she will be the subject of even less well defined procedures. Many local authorities use grading schemes to match tenants and dwellings (Gray 1976) but this procedure seems to be less important in SHDC. The housing stock is not officially graded at all and applicants are only officially graded if they are existing tenants with poor rent-paying records. Those with such a record will not be allowed to transfer until they have shown consistent rent-paying over a three-month period. However, an informal grading does occur during the home visit. The home visit report form includes a section wherein each room in the applicant's home is assessed for its cleanliness, decoration and tidiness; the grades are very good, good or average. The housing authority aims to be fairly open in this and tells the applicants how they have been graded. Although there is no formal use of this grading, it must colour the attitudes of the allocators.

The way in which the applicant is matched with a particular dwelling is very difficult to determine. To a certain extent it depends on the vacancies which become available when the applicant has reached a priority position. If a preferred house type in a preferred location becomes available and the applicant has no 'black marks' in either rent paying or the upkeep of his home, then a straightforward resolution to the allocation 'jigsaw puzzle' should be forthcoming. If this 'ideal home' is not available, then the allocation procedure is reduced to the housing official deciding what is the best option amongst the available suitable alternatives (also determined officially) which is not in demand from an applicant with a higher priority. Those with a poor record are likely to be faced with a more restricted choice, being unlikely to be offered a new property. At this point the allocation procedure, so carefully based on objective assessment, is dependent alone on the ability of the housing managers.

The applicant who has received an offer of rehousing may be in a dilemma, unless the offer is for the 'ideal home'. If it is refused, then there is no guarantee of receiving an improved offer next time. Also, after a second 'unreasonable' refusal the applicant will as a matter of policy not receive any further offers for a period of six months. This is subject to appeal to the elected members, a procedure that occurs rarely, and not at all in the twelve months prior to writing. Whether this indicates a high degree of satisfaction with the allocation procedure it is impossible to say, but an attempt to evaluate this will be made in the following chapter.

LOCATION AND ALLOCATION

The importance of location as a feature of rural housing need has been established in the previous chapters. It is given some, but limited, recognition in management policies in the SHDC as this section will demonstrate.

Both application forms allow for a statement of area preferences. The transfer list form allows four preferences to be expressed, while the waiting list allows two preferences and 'other acceptable' areas to be given. These are recognised in the allocation procedure at a number of stages. First, as suggested in chapter five, the pointing scheme allows between two and six points for those who live, or need to reside in, particular villages. The points are awarded in inverse relationship to the number of local authority properties in the village (not parishes). Hence villages with fewer than fifteen properties, such as Cornworthy or Wembury, have six points, while villages with between fifty and seventy properties, such as West Alvington, have two points. All the settlements with larger numbers of properties, including both the larger villages such as Yealmpton and the towns such as Totnes and Kingsbridge, are not awarded any points at all. The distribution of these points is shown in Figure 7.1. This is clearly a move to aid those living in areas where there are only small numbers of properties available and where, therefore, the opportunities for being rehoused locally are fewest. The map corresponds to the location of the more rural parts of the district and in view of the comments made in the previous chapter about the special needs of those living in these areas, this points criterion is a welcome addition to the allocation process. In relation to the total number of points allocated, however, this is likely to make only a marginal contribution, but it may be important in particular cases. The authority itself recognises this and at the time of writing was planning to strengthen the village points scheme.

Secondly, having been pointed, applicants are put into queues which, as was discussed earlier, are partly determined by location. The lengths of queues in different areas are likely to be variable. This, however, represents a passive feature of housing policies, reflecting the different opportunities in the sub-areas rather than an attempt to manage them. However, it should be noted that the very procedure of setting up sub-areas can complicate allocation. The boundaries are defined arbitrarily and could be redrawn with different parishes in a way which would change the lengths of the queues within them. Apart from administrative convenience, it is difficult to find any other rationale for this approach.

Finally, location obviously enters into the allocation of individual properties. Allocation of a property includes the allocation of proximity to friends, relatives, jobs, shops, services and neighbours. If property in the preferred parish is not available for letting to the priority applicant, then a decision has to be made as to whether there are any suitable alternatives. This is potentially contentious as it is very difficult to assess accurately

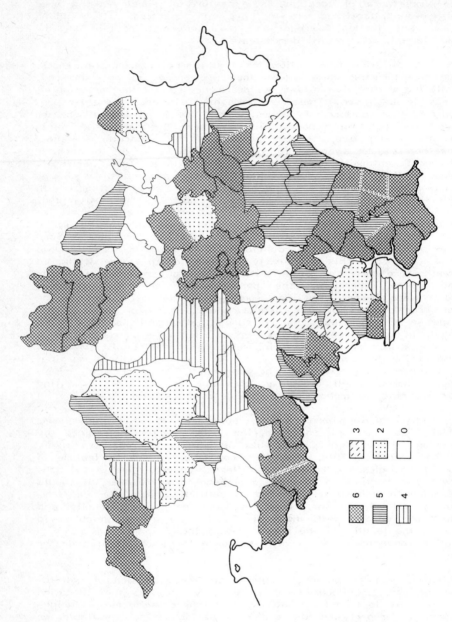

Figure 7.1: Additional waiting list points awarded for village location
Source: unpublished data SHDC

such a feature as the relative accessibility of different settlements. As in the more general question of allocation, the
allocation of particular locations rests largely in the hands of
the housing officials.

8 Social and territorial justice

CONCEPTS OF SOCIAL JUSTICE

In chapter five, the resources available to the housing authority – the housing stock – were examined, while chapter six assessed housing need and chapter seven examined the housing policies and procedures used to reconcile these. In this chapter, an attempt is made to evaluate the outcome of these management practices with reference to the now well-established concepts of social and territorial justice.

As previously discussed, the concept of social justice has been used by a number of researchers, such as Davies (1968) and Harvey (1973), and it is usually understood to mean an assessment of the effectiveness with which resources are being used to meet individual need, in the spirit of 'to each according to his needs' (Pinch 1979). In the context of local authority housing, two major features of this concept can be identified, which pose questions at quite different levels of explanation. The first concerns the way available resources are being used to meet the needs for housing. This is very much a short run perspective, almost looking at the day-to-day activities of the Housing Department, for in a short time span of a year or less, the actual supply of housing usually will change very little. Some new houses will become available but most lettings are dependent on vacancies being created in existing tenancies (although as was seen in chapter five, this was clearly not the case in South Hams in 1977). The major concern here is whether the available lettings are being used in an equitable manner relative to housing need in the area. In other words, do the procedures outlined in the previous chapters ensure that those who are in greatest need receive the available lettings? The second feature of social justice is the broader question of the total amount of resources devoted to housing. This is partly a question of taking a longer term view of the development of housing services, but more fundamentally, it raises questions about the control and accumulation of capital (for example, see Gray 1976b). It is not possible to develop this question properly here, but some attention will be paid to variations in the absolute levels of resources devoted to housing.

While the theme of social justice is an important one on its own, returning to the locational consideration of this book, it can be extended to the linked concept of territorial justice. This concept owes much to the work of Davies (1968) who saw territorial justice in terms of 'to each area according to the needs of the particular area'. This territorial approach has considerable value in the study of a rural area such as South Hams. On the·one hand, it has been observed that there are distinctive locational aspects of need, with important differences between the main settlements and the more rural areas. On the other hand, the allocation of resources is itself spatially uneven. Local authorities usually do not build spatially diffuse individual council houses but rather develop estates of varying sizes, which implies that areas will be differentially favoured. The concern of territorial justice, therefore, is the extent to which resources are allocated among the areas within South Hams in relation to local housing need. This approach could be applied in a formalised statistical approach, as used for example by Pinch (1978) in his work on local authority housing in Greater London, with needs and resources being correlated to identify the level of mismatch. This seems inappropriate here given the subtleties of the housing policies which are to be considered. Instead, as with social justice, the concept is used to give perspective to the analysis which follows.

There are two important reservations which have to be accepted with the adoption of this approach. One is that the existence of territorial justice need not necessarily imply that social justice also exists. Areas may be treated equitably but the individuals within them may not be. The other reservation is linked to this: territorial justice amongst the parishes of South Hams does not necessarily mean that there is territorial justice within them. This is particularly important in some of the larger settlements with several estates, which may not have equal treatment. This is a separate theme which is still being developed in the SHDC research. Finally, as with social justice, two levels of questions are involved - in the administration of available resources and in the determination of levels of expenditure on housing.

In the first instance, the analysis which follows will be structured successively by three linked questions. These are - who are housed, which houses are allocated, and where are these houses?

WHO? WHICH? AND WHERE?

Who are housed?

The rehousing practices of SHDC can partly be examined through the records of lettings. Table 8.1 summarises the main features of all lettings, whether new or relet properties, between 1976 and 1980. Information was available on lettings to the homeless, key workers, agricultural workers and the waiting list. It was not possible to differentiate between those with and without medical points on the housing register, and only for 1979/80 were there statistics available on the rehousing of transfer applicants. It is useful to omit the latter from this table anyway as the internal transfers both fill and create vacancies.

The data in this table are most revealing. Key workers and agricultural workers both represent fairly small numbers of those who are rehoused, and their combined total amounts to less than 4 per cent of all lettings between 1976 and 1980. However, there is some evidence that in the last two years there was an increase in the number of rehoused agricultural workers, perhaps as a result of the recent Rent (Agriculture) Act. Far more substantial are the lettings allocated to the homeless which increased dramatically from 16.2 per cent in 1976/7 to 29.7 per cent in 1979/80. Although the mean percentage is only about one-fifth of the total, in the last two years it has been nearer a third. This must be, at least in part, a result of the requirements of the Housing (Homeless Persons) Act of 1976. Combined with the initial evidence of an increase also in the number of agricultural workers to be rehoused, it seems that about a third of all lettings (net of transfers) are being used to fulfil the council's statutory obligations.

Table 8.1
Lettings (net of transfers) 1979-80

Percentages

Lettings to :	1976/7	1977/8	1978/9	1979/80	Total
Homeless	16.2	10.0	33.8	29.7	19.0
Key workers	2.4	1.1	3.4	3.7	2.2
Agricultural workers	1.6	0.5	2.9	4.1	1.7
Waiting List	79.8	88.4	59.8	62.5	77.1
Total	100.0	100.0	100.0	100.0	100.0
Total absolute no.	124	557	204	219	1104

Source: see Appendix A

Moving onto the remaining group, it is useful to compare waiting list and transfer list applicants. The only year for which this is possible is 1979/80 when there were 112 lettings for transfers compared to 137 for those on the waiting list out of a total of 331 lettings (including transfers). Therefore, very approximately equal numbers of lettings are made available to these two groups who received 33.9 and 41.5 per cent, respectively, of total lettings. Those on the waiting list seem to have experienced fairly mixed fortunes during this four-year period. Waiting list applicants are in a residual position in the allocation process, and therefore, in comparison to other groups, their opportunities for rehousing are more dependent on the total number of vacancies available. In turn this implies that their rehousing is considerably influenced by the level of completions of new dwellings. Thus, in the peak year of completions in South Hams, 1977-8, when net lettings were more than twice the level of any other year, waiting list applicants were allocated 88.4 per cent of all vacant properties. Since then, with a fall in the number of lettings and a rise in statutory rehousing needs, their share has fallen to about sixty per cent.

How far do these lettings represent social justice in rehousing? It is difficult to answer this question working simply from aggregate figures, but some comments are possible. First, the rehousing of the homeless and of those being evicted from tied agricultural cottages takes priority. This is a statutory obligation but these probably represent those in greatest need anyway. Secondly, key workers receive a measure of priority. It is questionable whether their housing needs are any greater than those on the waiting list, although obviously there are other considerations such as employment creation which support their priority. Thirdly, transfer list applicants receive priority over waiting list applicants. There are approximately twice as many waiting list applicants but they receive approximately the same number of lettings, so the probability of being rehoused is approximately twice as great for those on the transfer list. As was seen in chapter six, the needs of the former are certainly different and probably far more acute. In a simple comparison, then, there seems to be some inequity but as transfers also create new vacancies, no simple judgment is possible. The question of equity depends on the types of dwellings that are being allocated and these aggregate data do not allow for this to be considered. Finally, there are clear differences among waiting list applicants. Those with medical reasons, living in overcrowded or substandard properties, score the most points and presumably are more likely to be rehoused. Those further back in the queues with other needs, such as proximity to work or only moderate overcrowding, would seem to have very little chance of being rehoused.

Which houses, where?

Information on the properties available for letting was obtained from an analysis of the list of void (vacant) properties kept by the authority, covering the period April 1979 to April 1980. These lists are incomplete, but provide some information on the three main features of the houses allocated; these are accommodation type, number of bedrooms and location. Each of these can usefully be evaluated through a comparison with the characteristics of the total local authority housing stock.

Information on the types of property which are void is available for 150 cases, which is slightly less than half the total number of lettings known to have occurred during this period. Table 8.2 compares the voids with the overall types of property owned by the SHDC, described earlier in chapter five.

The largest number of available properties are houses, followed by flats and then bungalows. However, voids occur in flats and bungalows relatively more frequently than in houses. The frequency of voids in flats is to be expected given their unpopularity amongst transfer applicants (see chapter six), but the relatively large number of voids in bungalows is rather surprising. This may reflect the large number of elderly, single persons living in bungalows. They have lower life expectancies so voids may be created more frequently especially as there are less likely to be children or a married partner to whom the tenancy would be transferred.

Table 8.2
Types of properties void compared with the total housing stock

	Percentages	
Accommodation Type	Voids	Total housing stock
House	60.0	68.8
Flat	22.7	17.4
Bungalow	17.3	13.4
Total	100.0	100.0*

* There are also 18 non-classified dwellings.

The second feature of the void properties is the number of bedrooms and this is recorded in 148 cases. Table 8.3 shows that the largest number of voids occurs in three-bedroomed accommodation with approximately equal numbers in one- and two-bedroomed dwellings. Comparing these figures with those for the total housing stock, it will be seen that voids occur relatively more frequently in single bedroom dwellings and less frequently in two- and three-bedroomed dwellings. Therefore, as with the type of dwellings, some imbalances exist in the vacancies relative to the total housing stock available. It can be hypothesised but not proven that the relatively large number of single bedroomed dwellings available reflects the likelihood of changes in the circumstances of those occupying these properties; that is, the elderly and young couples starting a family.

Table 8.3
Number of bedrooms in void properties and the total housing stock

	Percentages	
No. of bedrooms	Voids	Total housing stock
1	26.4	18.0
2	23.6	26.6
3	49.3	54.1
4	0.7	1.3
Total	100.0	100.0

Finally, the locational features of the voids can be examined. Fortunately, there is information available on 256 of these, representing about three-quarters of all known lettings in this period. Figure 8.1 shows their distribution. There is a fairly wide spatial distribution of voids but there clearly is incomplete coverage. Only 35 of the 59 parishes with local authority houses seem to have had vacancies in this period (although some allowance has to be made for the missing information). Clearly the opportunities for being rehoused locally simply did not exist

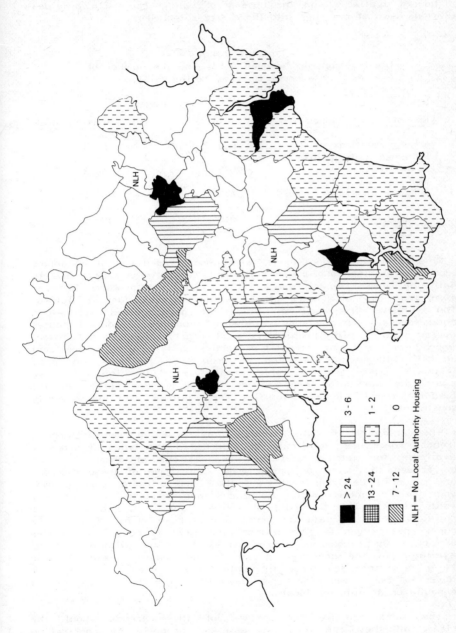

Figure 8.1: Distribution of void properties 1979–1980
Source: Appendix A

> 24

13 - 24

7 - 12

3 - 6

1 - 2

0

NLH = No Local Authority Housing

NLH

NLH

NLH

in all parishes in the period under review. To examine whether there is any consistent relationship between the total number of houses available and the number of voids, Table 8.4 provides a break down of parishes into three size categories.

Table 8.4
The relationship between voids and the number of available properties, by settlement type

| | Percentages | |
No. of l.a. houses	Voids	Total housing stock
4 major settlements	66.0	51.3
Parishes with 30–205 dwellings	29.3	40.3
Parishes with 29 or fewer dwellings	4.7	8.4
Total	100.0	100.0

This relationship does exist, with almost two-thirds of vacancies occurring in the four major settlements which have approximately half the total housing stock. In reality the problem is even more acute for a quarter of all voids occurred just in Totnes. The relative frequency of voids in medium-sized settlements and especially in parishes with small numbers of council houses is far smaller. The problem is particularly acute in the latter, where 8.4 per cent of all properties but only 4.7 per cent of all voids occur. As can be seen from the map, in many instances there are no voids whatsoever. This highlights once again the particular problems of the more rural areas of the district where the opportunities for mobility can be severely constrained.

The analysis in this section has revealed some alarming trends. There are significant imbalances in the types of property available for letting and in the locations of these. It can be argued that over a longer time span some of these discrepancies would be ironed out and that, for example, over a two-year period there would be far fewer parishes without any voids at all. This is true, of course, but it is not really the point. What these data do reveal is that in many of the more rural areas, even if an applicant has priority or a high number of points for rehousing, there may well be no suitable lettings available in the preferred parish for at least a year. A year is a long time for those in acute housing need and they may have to take some far less desirable alternative such as a caravan or an inferior location.

The social justice implications of these trends should be clear but they can only be assessed properly by considering the preferences of those who are in need, a theme that is returned to later.

ALLOCATION AND PREFERENCE

The analysis of allocations covered 230 matchings of individuals and dwellings which occurred between September 1979 and April 1980; these include sixty-five applicants from the transfer list and 165 other applicants, mainly from the waiting list but also including some homeless persons and agricultural workers. These were not always sufficiently clearly identified to allow the 'normal' waiting list applicants to be treated separately. The analysis was very time-consuming as it involved working from the names of allocated persons as stated in the reports to the Housing Committee; these then had to be traced back to the original application files. Hence a decision was taken to analyse the returns only of the eight months prior to and including April, 1980 rather than the full previous twelve months as had been originally planned. The numbers in the analysis are, therefore, smaller than had been hoped for (reduced even further in some instances by the large number who expressed no preferences) but do indicate some important trends. As in the previous section, three features of the allocation will be examined, being the type of dwelling, the number of bedrooms and the location.

The types of accommodation allocated to the two sets of applicants are shown in Table 8.5. This reveals that those on the transfer lists were more likely to be allocated houses and that those on the waiting list had a higher probability of ending up in a flat. Given the unpopularity of flats, transfer list applicants might be considered to be more favoured in the allocation pro-cedure. This can only be verified by examining the preferences of the two groups, which is difficult as preferences could only be traced for sixty-one of those on the waiting list and forty-six of those on the transfer list. The relatively small number of preferences that could be traced for the former is because they are not asked initially to state a specific house type preference on the housing register application forms. Their preferences are established, if at all, at a later date. Even with these small numbers there are revealing differences in the treatment of the two groups. While 96 per cent of transfer applicants were allocated their preferred type of accommodation, only 77 per cent of waiting list applicants were thus successful. The main difference between them is with respect to flats. Of the seven transfer list applicants who were allocated these, six had actually preferred them, while only nine of the fifteen waiting list applicants allocated flats had such preferences. In addition, thirty-one waiting list applicants who had not expressed any preference at all also ended up in flats.

In general then, transfer list applicants seem to be rather more favoured in this aspect of allocation as, presumably, they would not be inclined to transfer if they were not improving their housing or were not satisfied with an offer made to them. They are more likely than waiting list applicants to obtain their preferred dwelling type, and the latter are also more likely to get flats. Taylor (1979) in a study of Killingworth suggested that a model of allocations existed in which waiting list applicants were mainly housed in unpopular flats, and after a period of 'good conduct' or on proving medical reasons were allowed to transfer to other, more popular dwellings. Although no such extreme model exists in South Hams, it does seem that there are at least elements of this kind of procedure, in practice, if not in actual policy.

Table 8.5
Types of property allocated to applicants

Percentages

Accommodation Type	Waiting List	Transfer List
House	49.1	56.9
Flat	29.1	20.0
Bungalow	21.8	23.1
Total	100.0	100.0

A similar pattern exists with the allocated number of bedrooms (see Table 8.6). While approximately equal numbers of waiting list applicants were allocated to each of the bedroom size categories, almost a half of transfer list applicants were allocated to three-bedroom dwellings. Such a difference is to be expected as it was established earlier that transfer list applicants included more younger and probably expanding families who would need these larger dwellings. There is no significance in these allocations taken on their own. The preferences however place them in a different light; only 73 per cent (seventy-seven known preferences) of waiting list applicants compared to 93 per cent of transfer list applicants (forty-four known preferences) had the same preference and allocation. The main difference between them is with respect to those preferring two-bedroom dwellings. Whereas all the transfer list applicants were allocated their preferences, only fifteen out of thirty waiting list applicants were allocated two-bedroom accommodation; interestingly, ten out of the other fifteen were actually allocated more bedrooms than requested. In general then, transfer list applicants are more precisely served by the allocations procedure but those on the housing register do not fare badly. Some 73 per cent were allocated what they had asked for and only 6 per cent were given fewer bedrooms than they had requested.

When the locational aspect of allocation is considered, similar differences can be seen between the two groups. Table 8.7 shows the proportion of applicants who were allocated to their first preference or to one of their other preferences. As with the two previous tables there are again a number of individuals (sixty-one from the housing register and eleven transfers) for whom it has not been possible to establish preferences. Nevertheless, the differences are clear. Some 81 per cent of waiting applicants were allocated to one of their preferred parishes compared to 94.6 per cent of transfers, and the difference on first preferences is even greater. This is not to state that those on the waiting list are treated 'badly' in any sense, for two-thirds obtained their first choice parish and four-fifths obtained one of their preferred parishes. Nevertheless, the seemingly favoured status of transfers is again evident.

Table 8.6
Number of bedrooms allocated to applicants

Percentages

Number of bedrooms	Waiting List	Transfer List
1	35.8	20.0
2	30.9	30.8
3+	33.3	49.2
Total	100.0	100.0

Table 8.7
Parishes allocated to applicants

Percentages

Allocated to	Waiting List	Transfer List
First preference	67.0	87.3
Other preference	14.1	7.3
Other parishes	18.9	5.4
Total	100.0	100.0

The importance of locational considerations makes it worthwhile to consider this feature in more detail. In particular, the questions raised in chapter six about the need to be rehoused locally or to be moved to another parish can now be further examined. Table 8.8 gives a breakdown of preferences and allocations for these two types of rehousing. The first comment is that the percentages for all allocations reveal that those wishing to be rehoused locally are far more likely to be successful than those who would like to move to another parish. Of the latter, only about a half were allocated to their first choice parishes although they may have been rehoused in one of their other preferred areas. This again highlights the particular problems of those in more rural areas who would like to be transferred to more accessible locations.

The differences between the two groups of applicants are now even more distinctive. Of those wanting to be rehoused locally, all transfer applicants were successful and most waiting list applicants were successful. In contrast, while well over a half of transfer applicants were successful in inter-parish moves, this applied to less than half the waiting list applicants.

Table 8.8
Between and within parish preference and allocation

	Numbers				Per cent	
	Waiting List		Transfer List		Total	
Allocation	Within parish	Between parish	Within parish	Between parish	Within parish	Between parish
Allocated pre-ferred parish	50	22	37	11	92.5	49.3
Not allocated preferred parish	7	27	0	7	7.5	50.7
Total	57	49	37	18	100.0	100.0

Overall, two main features emerge from these data. On the one hand most applicants are allocated the type of property, the number of bedrooms and the parish that they expressed a preference for. This would indicate that a rough measure of social justice exists in the day-to-day management of housing in SHDC, given that need has been accurately assessed. On the other hand, those on the waiting list are rather less success-ful than those on the transfer list. They are most likely to secure flats or parishes that they did not specifically request. There is also an element of territorial injustice in that those wishing to move to a different parish are less successful than those wishing to be rehoused locally. In view of the locational aspects of need shown in chapter six, it may be suggested that there is greater injustice in the more rural areas. This is not to state that the managers of housing are directly at fault, for the earlier analysis of voids had shown considerable imbalances in the opportunities for rehousing. Obviously satis-factory rehousing cannot occur immediately if no suitable vacancies exist in the right place. Finally, it can be argued that many applicants will have changed their preferences after their initial statement of these, either because their own circumstances have changed or because they have become aware of other housing opportunities. Therefore, the argument continues, even the small proportion who do not seem to be allocated their preferred housing may in reality be quite well satisfied. This may be the case but the argument could of course also be turned on its head. In either case, without further information it is impossible to make an accurate allowance for this.

Back to the waiting list

In examining allocations, only the small proportion who actually are rehoused each year has been considered. Given the rate

132

of rehousing in 1979/80 (249 were rehoused from the waiting and transfer lists), it would take at least six years to clear the existing waiting and transfer lists. As large numbers of new applicants join the lists each year then, of course, the problem is far more substantial. This raises the question of who are likely to remain on the lists longer, perhaps never reaching the allocation stage? The answer with respect to the waiting list was partly outlined in the discussion of the points system in chapter seven. The largest number of points are awarded for medical reasons or for occupying substandard or overcrowded accommodation. Those suffering from only a 'moderate' degree of normative need in terms of any of these are likely to have very low priority for rehousing, as also are those needing to be rehoused in more accessible areas. However, the likelihood of being rehoused is also partly dependent on preference. Some types of houses and some areas are more or less popular than others. If these preferences then are compared to the accommodation which became void in the previous year, it should be possible to obtain an indication of the probability of rehousing. As in the earlier analysis, the focus is again on type of accommodation, number of bedrooms and location; for the first two features, it is only possible to consider those on the transfer list.

In Table 8.9 the voids and preferences for types of accommodation are compared. While the demand and supply of houses are more or less balanced in terms of proportions, there is a mismatch for bungalows and flats. In comparison to preferences there are too many flats and too few bungalows available. Those who would like, or are prepared to accept, flats are therefore more likely to be rehoused than those who prefer bungalows. Given the unpopularity of flats among transfer applicants and the relatively large number which become available, it is easy to understand why relatively large numbers of those on the housing register are rehoused in these. No queues exist as such for different types of accommodation, but waiting list applicants who find themselves at the head of a queue for a particular number of bedrooms will find that they may be offered a flat rather than the bungalow or house that they would prefer.

Table 8.9
Types of void accommodation and transfer
list applicants' preferences

| | Percentages | |
Type of accommodation	Voids	Preferences
House	60.0	60.3
Flat	22.7	15.7
Bungalow	17.3	24.0
Total	100.0	100.0

Imbalances between preferences and voids also exist for numbers of bedrooms (Table 8.10). There are relatively more voids than preferences in one- and three-bedroom dwellings and relatively fewer in two- and four-bedroomed accommodation. Although there is no actual queue for two-bedroom accommodation, this does approximate to the queue for families with a single child. As was seen in the previous section, transfer list applicants who preferred two-bedroom dwellings were all allocated this type, whereas only half of waiting list applicants were successful. Therefore, it is young families with one child who are on the waiting list who are most likely to be in the longest queues and to be obliged to accept more or fewer bedrooms than the number they would prefer.

Table 8.10
Numbers of bedrooms in void accommodation and transfer list applicants' preferences

Percentages

Number of bedrooms	Voids	Preferences
1	26.4	19.6
2	23.6	36.1
3	49.3	42.0
4+	0.7	2.3
Total	100.0	100.0

In considering the third feature, location, the data allow both sets of applicants to be examined. The locational imbalances are far smaller than those observed in respect of the other features. If voids and preferences are compared for settlements of different sizes (Table 8.11), then a remarkable balance is seen to exist. Slightly more voids occur in the larger settlements relative to preferences but really the differences are not substantial. Vacancies seem to occur with remarkable regularity in settlements of different sizes. This was obviously not the case two years earlier when there were large numbers of vacancies in new completions in the main settlements. Then applicants were faced with a choice between almost immediate allocation to one of the main towns or remaining on the waiting list in the hope of a vacancy occurring in the more rural areas. This is no longer the case for, on the evidence, the type of settlement preferred should make no difference to the length of time spent in the queues.

However, the actual balance of voids and preferences is far poorer than is indicated in this table. If the maps of preferences (Figures 6.3 and 6.4) and of voids (Figure 8.1) are compared, then it will be seen that there are 23 parishes which are the first preference of at least one applicant where no voids occurred in the last year. Voids do occur in the smaller settlements but in such small numbers that they have an erratic distribution. Whereas Blackawton and Bigbury, with 29 and 26 dwellings respectively, did not have a single void, Ringmore with 8 dwellings had one void and Sherford with only 6 dwellings had two voids. This confirms once again that those who prefer particular parishes in the more rural areas will find that reaching the front of a queue is no guarantee of being offered a suitably located dwelling.

Table 8.11
Voids in and preferences for different types of settlements

Settlement type	Percentages	
	Voids	Preference
4 major settlements	66.0	62.5
Parishes with 30–205 l.a. dwellings	29.3	32.7
Parishes with 29 or fewer l.a. dwellings	4.7	4.8
Total	100.0	100.0

With respect to all three features of housing, there are likely to be variations in the length of waiting time for rehousing. On the basis of this evidence, it seems that those who prefer bungalows and/or two bedrooms in the more rural areas are likely to face the longest waits. Those willing to accept a flat and/or any number of bedrooms in one of the major settlements will reach the allocation stage earlier.

ALLOCATION AND LOCATION

As the previous section revealed, locational preferences have an important role in queuing and allocation. The housing authority is aware of this and has introduced additional points for those preferring villages with small numbers of properties. These points are fairly marginal, however, compared to the numbers of points given under other headings and, even if they do bring an applicant to the head of a queue or to a priority position, this does not guarantee being rehoused in a preferred area. It is important, therefore, to consider the locational features of allocation in more detail and in particular to examine settlements of different sizes and the actual pattern of inter-parish allocation.

As is revealed in Table 8.12, preferences are most likely to match allocations if rehousing in one of the larger settlements has been requested. While 83.8 per cent of those wishing to be rehoused in Ivybridge, Kingsbridge, Dartmouth or Totnes were successful, only 45.5 per cent of those preferring particular parishes in more rural areas were successful. The reasons for this are two-fold. One is the distribution of voids, examined earlier, which makes it less likely that suitable vacancies

135

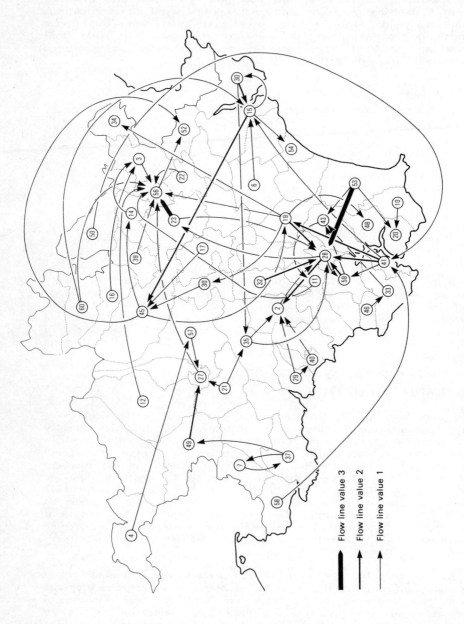

Figure 8.2: Inter-parish allocations 1979–1980
Source: Appendix A

Flow line value 3
Flow line value 2
Flow line value 1

will occur in rural areas; the second, that those in more rural areas are more likely to request inter-parish allocations, which are less successful than within-parish allocations.

Table 8.12
Type of settlement and the matching of first
preference and allocation

| | Transfer and waiting list applicants | | | |
| | | | Percentages | |
Settlement type	Preference equals allocation	Preference not equal to allocation	Total	Absolute Number
4 major settlements	83.8	16.2	100.0	99
Parishes with 30–205 l.a. dwellings	62.7	37.3	100.0	51
Parishes with 29 or fewer l.a. dwellings	45.5	54.5	100.0	11
Total	74.5	25.5	100.0	161

The key to successful rehousing then seems to be whether within-parish or between-parish mobility is needed. Almost all those on both the transfer and waiting lists were allocated to their preferred areas if they chose to stay in the same parish. Whether they are satisfied with location within the parish is a different question and one which cannot be investigated here. Those preferring to move to another parish were far less success-ful. Indeed, inter-parish rehousing represented only 31 per cent of all allocations (compared to 39 per cent of all preferences) so it is worth looking at these more closely. Figure 8.2 displays all the inter-parish allocations, irrespective of whether they are also preferred moves. The large number of moves makes it a little difficult to interpret this map but really there is a very simple pattern. The moves are strongly focused on the main settlements, especially on Kingsbridge and Totnes where, of course, most of the voids occurred. Most of the moves are also over fairly short distances so that allocations are contribut-ing to a centripetal movement into the main settlements from their immediate, more rural, surroundings. In contrast, there are a total of only seven moves out of the main settlements to more rural areas. Other than these urban-rural moves, there is only limited mobility within the more rural areas. It is possible to move between rural areas but only a few applicants actually achieve this. An even more dramatic picture is obtained if only the allocations of those rehoused in their preferred parishes are considered (see Figure 8.3). 'Successful' inter-parish movers to preferred areas are almost entirely to the major or the medium-sized settlements. Only three applicants who preferred a parish with twenty-nine or fewer council houses were actually successful in obtaining these moves.

In conclusion, it is possible to state that allocations better

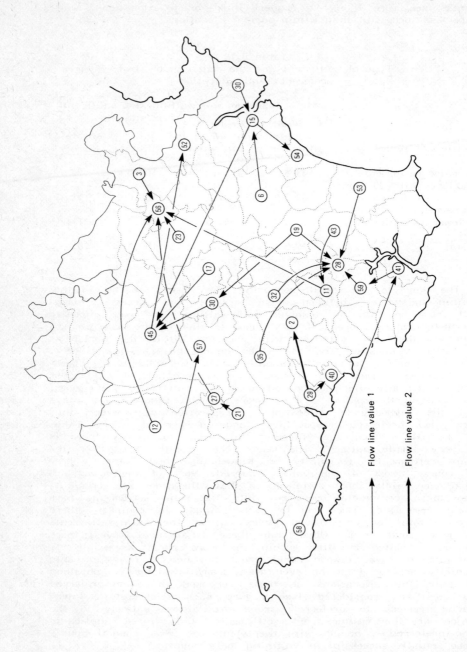

Figure 8.3: Inter-parish allocations to preferred parishes 1979–1930

Source: Appendix A

Flow line value 1

Flow line value 2

serve those who choose to remain in their local area or those who choose to move into the major settlements. This is partly a reflection of where the voids occur but it also raises a question as to whether the housing authority, deliberately or unconsciously, favours those who want to be rehoused locally (which the village points scheme suggests is the case). Movements between more rural areas do occur but they are infrequent and for those who are rehoused in a preferred area they are rare. It seems that those whose housing needs require a better or bigger house locally are probably best served by the allocations procedure. Those who, for reasons of accessibility, wish to move to a major or medium-size settlement also fare reasonably well. It is those applicants who prefer to remain in more rural parishes or, even more acutely, wish to transfer into a more rural parish who seem worst served. Strong elements of territorial injustice therefore seem to exist.

COUNCIL HOUSE SALES

In view of the locational aspect of housing need and allocation in rural areas, the sales of council houses which are imminent under the Right-to-buy legislation must cause special concern. The experience of SHDC is particularly relevant here for they operated an active sales campaign prior to the passing of the new national legislation. Up to August 1980, 208 houses were sold, representing about four per cent of the total housing stock. This is a high but not a remarkable level. However, the actual distribution of sales (see Figure 8.4) should be a matter of concern. In most parishes only a small proportion of the stock has been sold but there are some parishes where between 15 and 50 per cent of the stock has been sold. These are inevitably the more rural areas where there are initially only small numbers of dwellings. The two most notable examples are Ashprington and Diptford where half of the four and eight houses respectively available have been sold. Given the special problems that already exist for those with preferences for being rehoused in such rural areas, this pattern of sales is alarming. Effectively, the probability of voids occurring in such areas has been halved. As it happens, no voids occurred in these villages anyway in the period under review, so the future opportunities for rehousing in such areas are, to say the least, bleak.

It is not only the locational aspects of sales which are of concern. No information was readily available on the types of houses which have been sold but, if the preferences for rehousing are any guide, then in relation to the available stock it is bungalows which are most likely to be sold and flats which will be least in demand. As has been widely predicted (Building Trades Journal 1980; Schifferes 1980a; Watson 1980), this will lead to the loss of those dwellings which are in greatest relative demand. As with rural locations, those preferring or needing bungalows will find that the opportunities for satis-factory rehousing have been even further reduced.

Although the council does not seem unduly concerned with

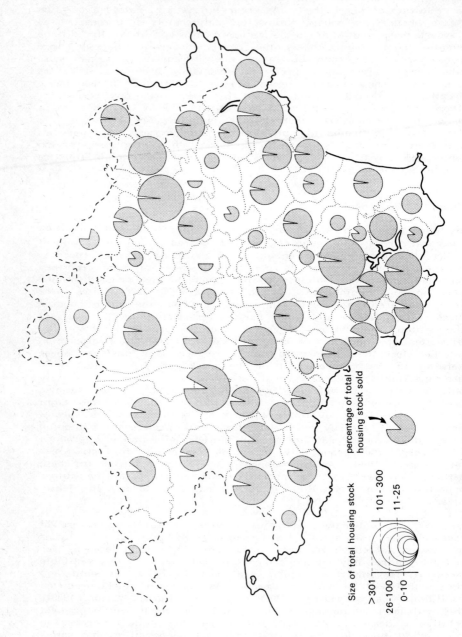

Size of total housing stock

percentage of total
housing stock sold

>301
101- 300
26-100
11-25
0-10

Figure 8.4: Council house sales before August 1980
Source: Appendix A

these consequences, it is very aware of another possible outcome of council house sales – the loss of homes to outsiders. In South Hams as in other areas with large numbers of second homes (Shucksmith 1981), there is concern that there will be 'no homes for locals'. The sale of council houses can increase this problem if ex-tenants later decide to resell their homes. In villages such as Ashprington and Diptford, where there are only a small number of council houses, this should prove to be relatively easy. If the houses are sold to outsiders, perhaps as second homes, then the housing opportunities for locals in all tenures will be reduced. This could happen in these villages or in other small clusters of council houses, especially in the attractive coastal areas, as illustrated by the map of second homes in chapter five. In view of this possibility, council houses were previously sold with a restrictive resale condition so that for a period of twenty-one years the Council had the first option to buy back the property if it was placed on the market. Furthermore, during the first five years, the resale price was fixed at the same level as the purchase price, which acted as a very effective barrier to early resale.

These safeguards, however, have been removed by the new Right-to-buy legislation. As was described in chapter three, the initial draft of the new legislation only placed resale restrictions on specially attractive areas which were AONBs, National Parks or protected coastal areas. Although such areas cover a considerable proportion of South Hams, as shown in chapter four, the resale restrictions adopted by SHDC stipulate only that the dwelling must be resold to a local person with at least three years' residence or employment in the area; therefore they are less restrictive than the Council's previous code of practice. The Housing Act (1980) allows tenants to buy their houses with a discount of 33 per cent on the market price for residents with a minimum qualifying period of three years, and up to a maximum discount of 50 per cent after twenty years' residence (Gilg 1981). A survey of 8 per cent of tenants conducted during the course of this research (see Appendix A) suggests that, in the SHDC area, large proportions may be eligible for substantial discounts if they were to decide to purchase their homes. 63 per cent were over the minimum qualification period to buy their homes, whilst one-quarter of those surveyed would receive the maximum discount of 50 per cent. This evidently provides a substantial potential market for sales at the same time as the legal restrictions on resale are being eroded.

The legislation did contain two possible 'let-out' clauses. First, the Secretary of State is also empowered to extend the resale restrictions to 'rural areas'. Therefore, SHDC, like many other district councils, requested that the Secretary of State should declare the whole of their area as rural. The Secretary of State replied in March 1981 accepting the arguments of SHDC and declaring most of the District as rural. However, there were four exceptions – Ivybridge, Kingsbridge, Dartmouth and Totnes – so that, in effect, about half of the housing stock remains unprotected. While this offers limited protection to locals in the more rural areas, the possibility still remains of large numbers of council homes eventually being resold to outsiders. As Totnes, Dartmouth and Kingsbridge are attractive towns, this is no mean threat.

SECTION D

CONCLUSIONS

9 Rural housing and the public sector: the future?

A number of conclusions can be drawn from the research reported in this book, and, in addition, certain policy recommendations can be suggested. Inevitably, a number of the conclusions and recommendations will tend to be specific to the South Hams study area, but others are of a broader nature and will be of relevance to many of the authorities involved in housing management in rural areas. In chapter one, it was suggested that the research is not specifically concerned with the physical condition of the housing stock – this is of almost incidental interest rather than a central focus. Much information concerning amenities and the like can be gleaned from the census and will no doubt be analysed in some detail when the 1981 Census results become available. The research has instead taken as its major concern matters of access to local authority housing in the case study area: physical, social and economic access. In particular, it has considered the ways in which the activities of local authority housing managers, as critical personnel in the housing allocation process, can influence the life chances of residents in local areas by their determination of housing priorities, location and accessibility.

The book began with a survey of changing rural conditions and eventually reached the conclusion that accessibility to a wide range of services and opportunities is a major problem in rural areas. From a recognition that different tenure groups have different problems (Dunn et al 1981), the focus moved to persons within local authority housing and, more importantly, those wishing to move into local authority accommodation or within this sector. The relative ease with which this can be done and the appropriateness of accommodation allocated to the needs of individual households must be a measure of the success of housing policy.

Housing policy is, of course, only determined in part by local managers in their allocative activities and their exercise of discretionary powers. It is also influenced from a higher level by the philosophy of the national political system and government of the day towards publicly-provided housing which can determine the resources devoted to it. As a result, certain conclusions will relate to this theme, the potential friction between local administrators (under pressure to solve 'local' housing problems) and national political directives which mean that the resources allocated to the public sector for housing provision vary from time to time.

THE STUDY AREA

The South Hams is a fairly typical rural area: conservative-minded, with a high dependence on agriculture and tourism for its income and employment. Local authority housing accounts for only some 18 per cent of the total housing stock and this proportion is decreasing as parts of the stock are sold off gradually. Possibly less typical of rural areas, the SHDC now has a Housing Department which is well-equipped in qualified personnel and which should be able to take an overview of the whole district. Yet still there remain problems in the length of the waiting list and also in transfer list allocations.

The research therefore delved into the records of the Council's Housing Department to examine the nature of its allocation process. It is evident that the tenants and prospective tenants themselves are not involved in this process, apart from their limited activity of filling in application forms for housing. Therefore, an area of deficiency in the research can be pointed out, namely that the attitudes, aspirations and behaviour of tenants are not being investigated except through the restricted media of application and transfer forms and lists.

Due to the relatively small number of vacancies which occurred annually in the declining housing stock, applicants of any type (for transfer and for first accommodation) were relatively unlikely to be housed quickly. Instead, those in the categories for whom the Council is obliged to find housing (such as the homeless) are more likely to be housed in a relatively short space of time. Transfer list applicants appear, on the whole, to be better served in terms of their preferences for location, type and size of housing than are general waiting list applicants. It is possible therefore to question whether a sufficient priority is being given to waiting list applicants; perhaps it is not.

However, at times, waiting list applicants fared quite well. This is particularly true of the period of rapid provision of local authority dwellings during the mid-1970s. This shows that, given the political will and the economic resources, waiting lists can be considerably reduced in a relatively short period of time. In times of economic stringency, waiting list applicants fare relatively more poorly than other categories to whom housing was allocated, so their fortunes do tend to vary with absolute levels of provision. This does not bode well for the future of allocations to such applicants as, today, re-lets rather than new lettings are the main resource available for the allocation and satisfaction of need.

SOCIAL AND TERRITORIAL JUSTICE?

At a local scale, questions of social justice arise from these remarks. It certainly appears that certain persons, notably transfer list applicants, were more likely to obtain the type and size of property they required. They were more likely to obtain a house (waiting list applicants were more likely to be allocated a flat). 96 per cent of them were successful in their preferences but this might well be expected because, if not offered properties they desired, they might have refused to transfer. This harks back to the suggestion in chapter six

146

that transfers are more likely to be a 'fine tuning' response to changing housing needs over time. However, almost two-thirds of waiting list applicants also obtained their first choice of house size and so the housing authority is relatively successful here, too.

A rough measure of social justice in allocation can thus be suggested as most applicants obtain more or less the type of housing they want. The major proviso is, however, with regards to territorial justice, a major matter in rural areas. The majority of applicants wished to move into one of the larger settlements in the South Hams, but an important minority wished to move to other rural areas. The majority of allocations were in the four main settlements as well, and this is influenced by a number of factors. First, the majority of the stock (and virtually all new houses) was built in the main settlements (apart from Dartmouth). Secondly, the greatest numbers of voids occurred, as a result, in these locations. In addition, a smaller number of voids than might have been expected occurred in some of the smaller parishes and villages so, frequently, there were no opportunities at all for allocation to them. Territorial injustice was thus almost inevitable in a number of cases where there was no possibility of allocation to desired locations.

This raises a number of more general matters relating to social and territorial justice. The first question, posed in chapter eight, relates to the efficiency of use of existing resources to meet the housing needs of the District. Do those in greatest need obtain what they require? Shucksmith (1981) suggests that, in the absence of government intervention in the allocation of housing, the rural housing market is neither efficient nor equitable. This case-study suggests that, with a co-ordinated housing management, a degree of social justice in allocation can be achieved but this is tempered with a number of notable shortcomings. For local waiting list applicants, the statutory obligations to rehouse various other categories of people can mean a long wait to receive, eventually inappropriate accommodation. Relatively few key workers may be brought in to disrupt local allocations, but almost 30 per cent of allocations by 1979-1980 were to persons legally defined as 'homeless'.

This leads to the second major question concerning social justice, and this relates to the adequacy of investment in local authority housing. The large number of statutory allocations in recent years (up to one-third of the total) must mean some deficit in supply of housing for other persons in less urgent (but still considerable) normative need. Immediately, the national policy of retrenchment in local authority building can be blamed. It has already been illustrated that a relatively modest programme of expansion of the local authority housing stock can considerably reduce waiting lists (and produce social justice, even if territorial justice may be questioned due to the location of the new estates). However, now, even if the local authority were to wish to proceed with large building campaigns, this would not be permitted. Therefore, the national-scale political economy conditions are felt very rapidly at the local level, when a small housing stock becomes eroded rather than increased.

Two more matters are thus raised. First, the questions of the aims of social policy: as Dunn et al (1981) point out, and as suggested in chapter one, the aims of social policy should be to ensure that those who come late are at least assured of a reasonable deal. This is not the case, sadly. Latecomers who have only moderate levels of normatively-evaluated need are now unlikely to be successful in obtaining a local authority dwelling. In reality, their need may be much greater than that of some persons who successfully apply for transfer between local authority homes. In chapter six, major life-cycle changes and present unsuitable accommodation were seen to be responsible for many applications to the waiting list, whilst a majority of transfer list applicants frequently sought only to make apparently smaller improvements to their present housing circumstances. However, the latter were more likely to be appropriately suited in many cases than were the former. So, the adequacy of social policy can be questioned here.

Secondly, the matter of housing stock and its reduction by the sale of council-owned dwellings is of great national and local importance. Nationally, the reduction of direct public involvement in housing provision may be lamentable but, locally, the mattern can assume great significance. In chapter eight, it was shown that the local authority stock of some parishes and villages could effectively be reduced by sales, possibly to the point when either no voids come up or no houses remain in public ownership. The small public housing stock in many villages means that those houses that are council owned are attractive for purchase. The SHDC has traditionally been quite fair to tenants and to future householders in its attitude to sales but the new legislation may well give it less protection than it had previously, to refuse to sell where it does not want to. As a result, it may be observed that national political decisions can act to create friction between central and local government and between local authority housing managers and local residents and would-be residents of their dwellings.

The suggestion that local authorities in locations such as the South Hams should build more houses in order to counter sales, second home ownership and planning policies which restrict development to designated centres is, of course, not feasible given current central government policies. This research supports the conclusions drawn by Shucksmith (1981) that there is a relative shortage of local authority housing in rural areas both when viewed in terms of expressed need (waiting lists) and when compared with other areas of the country. This shortage is exacerbated by a lack of building (so that the stock inevitably ages without replacement) and by sales (so that the ageing stock becomes yet smaller).

In chapter two, a major case was made that the problems of rural accessibility might be worsened by inappropriate distribution of housing. Housing is fundamental to people's lives and certain parts of village populations may be directly dependent upon the local authority to provide an adequate level of housing near to their work, family and friends. In some villages, this proportion will be small and it is important that their opportunities for obtaining housing locally are not reduced either by sales of stock or by inadequate allocation procedures. This research suggests that it is persons wishing to be housed or rehoused in the smaller settlements who are least likely to be suited either because vacancies just do not occur in the appropriate locations or the types of dwellings they require just do not exist where they are needed. However, the basic question posed in chapter two of whether the costs to society of maintaining small rural settlements can be justified remains largely unresearched and unanswered.

This problem of small housing stocks cannot be redressed at present due to the lack of building but, possibly, some substitution of roles can be achieved if the housing authority is able to stimulate enough activity, for example, of non-profit making housing associations in its area. Whether locals will be able to afford these is a matter of considerable concern, however, given the low wages and unemployment of areas such as the South Hams. Ironically, central government has contradictory aims for local authority housing managers : to provide statutory housing for certain groups yet to sell their housing stock and reduce the chance of meeting even statutory obligations. How this conundrum will eventually work out remains to be seen in many different localities.

The assessment of need

Certain more minor policy recommendations can be made, mainly with regard to the methods adopted to assess need, the critical matter of the pointing scheme, explained in detail in chapter seven. It is certain that some quasi-objective pointing system such as that which is currently in use by SHDC and many other local housing authorities is preferable to the patronage system under which local councillors decide upon allocation 'on merit'. However, minor improvements could be made even to the new pointing scheme, mainly with regard to the weighting given for accessibility. The scheme would appear quite sound for an urban area but, as explained in chapter two, the related matters of housing and accessibility to a range of goods and services is crucial in a rural area where mobility and transportation can be very restricted. Only up to a maximum of six points are awarded for those who need to live in villages with very few local authority dwellings, which will tend to be a small number in relation to the total number of points allocated. This is under review at present and any strengthening of the importance attached to 'accessibility' (even if only indirectly measured) is to be welcomed. It has been clearly seen that the majority of successful applicants for housing were either housed locally in their own parish or in one of the four largest towns. There are certainly undertones of territorial injustice for those needing to move from one rural parish to another but, without the provision of additional housing stock, this is very hard to combat.

Similarly, in the pointing scheme, some points seem, paradox-
ically, more important than others. Notably, people with the
full number of medical points are (probably justly) allowed
very high priority in allocations. However, relatively low priority
is given to length of residence (above the qualifying period)
in the South Hams. These points only count if all else is equal
and residents of longstanding could justifiably feel aggrieved
by apparent 'queue-jumping' by outsiders. The balance of
the argument here, however, is very difficult to decide. Should
locals in less normative need receive a higher priority in housing
allocation than persons of shorter length of residence but with
greater need? Local ratepayers may feel that they have contribu-
ted to the cost of the local housing stock but, immigrants from
abroad aside, most applicants will have been paying rates
in some part of the country and so the matter should eventually
even itself out. The grading system for applicants by housing
visitors plays a relatively less important part than in many
other authorities. It is ostensibly fair and applicants are informed
of their grading and can appeal if they disagree with it. SHDC
seems relatively progressive in this respect.

Thus, apart from relatively minor suggestions regarding
the current methods of pointing, this research tends to validate
the details of the system. However, the locational imbalances
in the housing stock, its over-concentration in the main settlements and the sheer lack of housing (for example, for the
elderly and in certain parishes) make even a basically sound
pointing scheme almost inevitably inequitable to some parties.

DIRECTIONS FOR FUTURE RESEARCH

A major revelation uncovered during this research is the fact
that, as yet, very little is known about basic features of rural
housing and rural problems. Research is, with some exceptions,
still at the stage at which gross general statements can be
made based on rather slim empirical knowledge. During the
course of this project it became increasingly evident that a
thorough review of local authority involvement in rural housing
must soon be undertaken. Newby et al (1978) hint at the historic
factors underlying the development (and hindrances to development)
of rural council housing but there is, as yet, no systematic
appraisal of the legislative and quantitative development of
rural local authority housing comparable to those which exist
for urban areas. The point has been emphasised that very little
is known of the political economy of rural housing and how
this governs matters such as investment and completion rates.

During the course of writing the empirical chapters, a number
of lesser avenues for future research became evident. For example,
some degree of spatial disaggregation of results is essential
for future projects upon these lines. In chapter eight, it was
pointed out that territorial justice and social justice are not
necessarily synonymous. Areas may well be treated equally

whilst individuals or estates within them may receive different treatment. Who? What? and Where? were terms emotively used but which illustrate that matters can be looked at on a variety of spatial scales. Is there, for instance, equal treatment within parishes as well as between parishes for applicants of all sorts? Only by refined spatial analysis can such questions be answered.

Evidence was found to show high rates of applications (as well as high allocations) for housing in the major settlements. However, from research such as the present, it is not possible to elicit whether these applications are merely responses to known (or perceived) opportunities or whether they reflect genuine desires for centrality and access to larger settlements. An impressive visual focus on the major settlements was provided by maps such as Figures 6.5 and 6.6, but is this expressed need (shown in the application forms, the only 'need' for which information was available) an accurate reflection of felt need? In reality, would applicants prefer to apply for housing outside the main centres if they felt that there was any hope of being allocated it?

This introduces some of the limitations associated with the present type of analysis. The managerialist approach adopted is unable to distinguish the attitudes, motivations or felt needs of applicants or tenants. A tenancy survey was, in fact, conducted for an approximately eight per cent sample of residents in local authority housing and information on the types of persons actually in residence was gleaned from this (Phillips and Williams 1981b). However, if time and resources permitted, it would certainly be desirable to leaven with some behavioural detail these managerialist perspectives, by interviewing applicants and transfer applicants to discover their real motivations and aspirations.

Only by additional behavioural research can the real problem of accessibility and its relationship to the location of housing be assessed. Do people decide not to change jobs because they are aware that they will face severe housing problems in rural areas? Does the local authority sector in itself prove to be a sort of 'housing trap' from which escape is difficult? Longitudinal research is required to supplement the knowledge of expressed needs because this provides only a limited measure of the way in which the housing market affects individuals. The behavioural and the managerial scales of analysis must essentially be seen as complementary rather than separate.

Research such as that illustrated by this book, at the managerialist level, only considers outcomes and the rules under which decisions are made. It does not give any indications whether the housing managers themselves feel the methods of allocation to be fair or adequate for, as individuals, they will have their own ideas and ideals. As the professionals in the rural housing field, it would be very desirable for some future research to focus more directly upon their behaviour and attitudes.

In the same line of reasoning, but with regard to the housing stock itself, is it, for example, sufficient merely to indicate the numbers, types and locations of local authority houses that are sold? From such information, only inferences can be drawn as to what happens to this stock. It will, in the future be very valuable to follow through some longitudinal 'case histories' of houses sold. Do they become second homes? Do they revert, as they sometimes should, to local authorities? Why do tenants buy some houses and not others? How long do they remain in the hands of original purchasers? All these vistas are opened up now as sales increase over the years. Data on this important question should be gathered without delay.

What of the alternatives in rural housing? Will local authority participation in housing associations act as a sufficient substitute for direct provision of housing? Or will housing associations just provide another form of unaffordable owner-occupancy for many rural dwellers? Do housing associations help those in housing need in rural areas? Again, the basic research must soon be undertaken to provide at least some guidance for local and national policies.

What of the local politicians under whose auspices policy is formulated? Newby et al very rightly illustrate the need for an analysis of their activities and political leanings insofar as they affect their involvement in rural local authority housing. For such a study, a more subtle blend of political analysis than was possible using the data in this book would be essential. The political composition of local councils and the activities of influential individuals on council sub-committees would all require very detailed research, much of which would rely on personal observations and personal contacts rather than on 'hard' data and records, published or unpublished. This current research would have been much enlightened had a 'window' been available through which to view council policy in the formulation but, sadly, such an opportunity did not present itself. The access actually allowed to otherwise restricted data was in any case a rare enough event.

In conclusion, in this book, the authors have attempted to analyse in academic terms what is often not an 'academically pure' exercise. Pragmatism and local circumstances must inevitably colour any managerial decisions and hence influence any conclusions which are reached. However, it is evident that this type of research demands replication in many other rural settings in order to determine the universality of findings. it may be hoped that, as a result of studies such as this, managers of rural local authority housing will at least reconsider matters of social and territorial justice in their own localities. This by itself would be justification for such research.

APPENDIX

Appendix

This appendix is intended to provide a summary of the methodology adopted and data sources utilised in the South Hams Housing
Project. The summary is organised in the same sequence as the
working papers referred to in the bibliography (Phillips and
Williams 1980a, 1980b, 1980c, 1981a, 1981b). Consultation of these
working papers will provide further details of data sources and
tabulations as well as additional maps. The subjects of the working papers are as follows:

1. Local authority housing stock, South Hams
2. Local authority tenants' applications to transfer in the South
    Hams
3. Housing in the South Hams. context for housing
4. Applications for housing to South Hams District Council
5. Sample tenancy survey

The bulk of the data in Working Papers 1 to 4 were collated from
various sources within South Hams District Council (SHDC). The
1971 Census also provided a certain amount of 'benchmark' information which both the SHDC and this project have utilised on
occasion. At the time that this research was carried out, up to
mid-1980, the SHDC Planning Department was collating a range
of demographic, economic and social data for the draft District
Plan. This provided invaluable background information for the
project, although subsequently the draft has largely been super-
seded by the final version intended for publication. The bulk
of the housing information was, however, gathered and compiled
by the authors' research assistant, Geoffrey Brown, from the
sources outlined below, within various departments of SHDC. He
also conducted the home interviews of local authority tenants upon
which Working Paper 5 (Tenancy Survey) is based.

1 Local authority housing stock

Sources: House records held by Technical Services Department
    which give address, number of rooms and household
    facilities for each local authority dwelling. These are
    mainly intended as maintenance records.

Tabulations: Provided at three spatial scales (district level,
    housing district level and parish level) for the following:
    Numbers and types of dwellings.
    Bedroom numbers.
    Dates of construction of dwellings. ·

Specifications: Information was available for 4633 dwellings
    held by SHDC (Dec.1979), with data partially lacking in
    certain instances: type of dwelling (11 cases), number
    of bedrooms (14 cases), dates of construction (4 cases).

155

2   Local authority tenants' applications to transfer

Sources: The original application forms of tenants requesting transfers, as held by Housing Department, SHDC, in March 1980. The main topics upon which tenants were required to provide information are listed earlier in Table 7.3.

Tabulations: Provided at parish and district level for the following:
Transfer applicants (ages, family sizes, parish distribution, length of time on transfer list, length of residence at present address, car ownership and places of work).
Present housing circumstances (type of present accommodation, number of bedrooms and living rooms).
Choice of accommodation (type, bedrooms, parish).
Crosstabulations of present and preferred accommodation, type and bedroom numbers.
Reasons cited in support of transfer requests.
Crosstabulations of reasons and preferred accommodation, and of intra-parish and inter-parish requests.
Refusals of offers to transfer (reasons and crosstabulations with present accommodation).
Patterns of spatial mobility (intra-parish and inter-parish mobility, and relationship to the total l.a. housing stock).

Specifications: Total number of transfer requests 531, of which, only 16 per cent were registered prior to October 1976. Of the data used in this book, the main missing items of information were: type of present accommodation (39 cases), number of bedrooms (5 cases), choice of accommodation type (72 cases), choice of number of bedrooms (57 cases) and choice of parish (34 cases).

Note: The applications to transfer can only be considered to be accurate at the date of original registration as the domestic circumstances and the preferences of applicants may change. In addition, these data do not include the tenants wishing to exchange dwellings within SHDC or to transfer to another local authority, although these are numerically insignificant. Nevertheless, these records do provide good indications of the main features of the then current housing circumstances, motivations and preferences of those wishing to transfer within SHDC.

3 Housing in the South Hams: context for housing

This working paper presents information on three major topics with data drawn from a variety of sources indicated below.

Topic	Tabulations	Sources	Specifications
Social and demographic details	population change socio–economic groups	C; DDP C; DDP	
Housing	tenure occupancy rates second homes	C; DDP C; DDP SWEPC	 Unpubl. data from 1973 Survey; unavailable for Plympton RDC
	housing stock private and l.a. completions	C; DDP PD; TSD	 Available for period Jan. 1974 – Oct.1979; includes information on bedroom numbers
	accommodation for the elderly	C; HD; TSD	Information on sheltered housing and accommodation designated for the elderly
Housing management	void properties	HD records	27 voids lists available for year beginning April, 1979 (maximum 256 cases)
	lettings	HD records and returns	Available for period April 1976 – April 1980
	homelessness	HD returns	Available for year beginning April 1, 1979 (lettings to homeless = 58)
	allocations	HD records; TL; WL	Available for period Sept. 1979 – April, 1980 (maximum of 230 cases)
	council house sales	HD records	Available until Aug. 1980

Key to data sources:
C   = 1971 Census of England and Wales
DDP   = draft SHDC District Plan
SWEPC   = South West Economic Planning Council
PD   = SHDC Planning Department
TSD   = SHDC Technical Services Department
HD   = SHDC Housing Department (internal records plus returns
                                    to Housing Committee)
TL   = Transfer list application forms, Housing Department
WL   = Waiting list application forms, Housing Department

4 Applications for housing to South Hams District Council

Sources: Records of applications for housing to SHDC. These records were updated from late 1979 when a complete re-pointing of all existing and new applicants to the housing register was conducted by the Housing Department.

Tabulations: Applicants (ages, family sizes, present addresses, year of application, length of time at present address, employment status, social class, places of work, disabilities).
Present housing circumstances (type and tenure of present accommodation, number of bedrooms and household facilities possessed).
Crosstabulations of family size and type and tenure of accommodation, and number of bedrooms.
Choice of accommodation (parish).
Reasons in support of application and preferred area.
Patterns of spatial mobility (intra-parish and inter-parish mobility, and relationship to the total l.a. housing stock).

Specifications: Total number of applications up to March 1980 was 1000.
Of the data used in this book, the main missing information on applications was: present residence (14 cases), year of application (6 cases), length of time at present address (21 cases), employment status (49 cases), present type of accommodation (39 cases), present tenure (48 cases), choice of parish (82 cases).

Note: As in Working Paper 2, applications to the housing register can only be considered to be accurate at the time of original registration. Therefore, these data do give a good picture of the circumstances and needs of all applicants to SHDC in the early 1980s when the repointing exercise was carried out.

5   Sample tenancy survey

Source: An 8 per cent household survey of local authority tenants in SHDC. The sample was drawn from parishes selected to provide a variety of l.a. housing stock sizes and locations across the district, including the main towns. The survey was conducted in early 1980. The survey parishes and the samples as a percentage of all l.a. dwellings in each were as follows: Bigbury (50%), Loddiswell (24%), South Pool (67%), Bickleigh (100%), Brixton (16%), lvybridge (10%), Holne (75%), Ugborough (23%), Dartmouth (9%), Totnes (9%), Kingsbridge (9%), Salcombe (12%).

Tabulations: House types, number of bedrooms, dates occupancy and tenancy commenced, family sizes, ages, social class, tenants on transfer list and supporting reasons.
Crosstabulations of family sizes and type of house and number of bedrooms.

Specifications: Survey size was 325 respondents, equivalent to approximately 8 per cent of dwellings still held by SHDC in mid 1980.
Missing information: House type (6 cases), bedroom numbers (6 cases), date of occupancy (13 cases), family sizes (1 case), ages (4 cases), and social class (2 cases).

BIBLIOGRAPHY
AND
INDEX

Bibliography

Ambrose, P., *The Quiet Revolution: Social Change in a Sussex Village 1871–1971*, Chatto and Windus, London 1974.

Aughton, H., 'Demolition job planned on housing expenditure', *Roof*, 5, 1980.

Ball, M., 'British Housing policy and the house building industry', *Capital and Class*, 4, 1978.

Bates, M. and Cudmore, B.V., *Country Planning: A Restudy*, Institute of Agricultural Economics, University of Oxford, Oxford 1975.

Beresford, T., *We Plough the Fields*, Pelican, Harmondsworth 1975.

Berry, F., *Housing: the Great British Failure*, Charles Knight, London 1974.

Bielckus, C.L., Rogers, A.W. and Wibberley, G.P., *Second Homes in England and Wales*, Studies in Rural Land Use No. 11, Wye College, University of London, London 1972.

Bird, H., 'Residential mobility and preference patterns in the public sector of the housing market', *Transactions of the Institute of British Geographers*, New Series 1, 1976.

Blacksell, M. and Gilg, A., *The Countryside: Planning and Change*, Allen and Unwin, London 1981.

Blaxter, M., 'Social class and health inequalities' in Carter, C.O. and Peel, J. (eds.), *Equalities and Inequalities in Health*, Academic Press, London 1976.

Boddy, M., 'The structure of mortgage finance: building societies and the British social formation', *Transactions of the Institute of British Geographers*, New Series 1, 1976.

Boddy, M., *The Building Societies*, Macmillan, London 1980.

Bollom, C., *Attitudes and Second Homes in Rural Wales*, Social Science Monograph No. 3, University of Wales Press, Cardiff 1978.

Bradshaw, J., 'The concept of social need', *New Society*, 496, 1972.

Brockway, F., *Hungry England*, Gollancz, London 1932.

Brotherston, Sir John, 'Inequality: is it inevitable?' in Carter, C.O. and Peel, J. (eds.), *Equalities and Inequalities in Health*, Academic Press, London 1976.

Building Societies Association, *Housing Facts*, The Building Societies Association, Park Street, London 1980.

Building Trades Journal, 'Implications of the right to buy council houses', *Building Trades Journal*, 180, 4 July 1980.

Burns, J.T., 'Fair gradings – for houses and tenants', *Municipal and Public Services Journal*, 87, 1979.

Butler, A., 'Profile of the sheltered housing tenant', *Housing*, 16, June 1980.

Byrne, D., Williamson, B. and Fletcher, B., *The Poverty of Education*, Martin Robertson, London 1975.

Campbell, M., *Capitalism in the UK: A Perspective from Marxist Political Economy*, Croom Helm, London 1981.

Cartwright, A. and O'Brien, M., 'Social class variations in health care and in the nature of general practitioner consultations' in Stacey, M. (ed.), *The Sociology of the NHS*, Sociological Review Monograph, No.22, University of Keele, Keele, Staffordshire 1976.

Central Housing Advisory Committee, *Council Housing : Purposes, Procedures and Priorities*, HMSO, London 1969.

Chambers, J.D. and Mingay, G.E., *The Agricultural Revolution 1750–1880*, Batsford, London 1966.

Cherry, G.E. (ed.), *Rural Planning Problems*, Leonard Hill, London 1976.

Clark, D. and Unwin, K., 'Community information in rural areas: an evaluation of alternative systems of delivery' in Shaw, M. (ed.), *Rural Deprivation and Planning*, Geo Books, Norwich 1979.

Clements, L.M., 'The demise of tied cottages – Rent (Agriculture) Act 1976', *The Conveyancer and Property Lawyer*, 42, 1978.

Cloke, P.J., 'An index of rurality for England and Wales', *Regional Studies*, 11, 1977.

Cloke, P.J., 'Changing patterns of urbanisation in rural areas of England and Wales, 1961 – 1971', *Regional Studies*, 12, 1978.

Cloke, P.J., *Key Settlements in Rural Areas*, Methuen, London 1979.

Cloke, P.J., 'New emphases for applied rural geography', *Progress in Human Geography*, 4, 1980a.

Cloke, P.J., 'The key settlement approach: the theoretical argument', *The Planner*, 66, 1980b.

Cloke, P.J., 'Key settlements', *Town and Country Planning*, 49, 1980c.

Cloke, P.J. and Park, C.C., 'Deprivation, resources and planning: some implications for applied rural geography', *Geoforum*, 11, 1980.

Community Development Project, *Whatever Happened to Council Housing?*, CDP Information and Intelligence Unit, London 1976.

Community Development Project, *The Costs of Industrial Change*, Community Development Project, Inter-Project Editorial Team, London 1977.

Coppock, J.T. (ed.), *Second Homes: Curse or Blessing*, Pergamon, Oxford 1977.

Cullingworth, J.B., *Housing and Local Government*, Allen and Unwin, London 1966.

Cullingworth, J.B., *Essays on Housing Policy: The British Scene*, George Allen and Unwin, London 1979.

Davies, B.P., *Social Needs and Resources in Local Services*, Michael Joseph, London 1968.

Deane, P., *The First Industrial Revolution*, Cambridge University Press, Cambridge 1965.

Dear, M., 'A paradigm for public facility location', *Antipode*, 6, 1974.

Department of the Environment, *British Cities: Urban Population and Employment Trends 1951-71*, Department of the Environment, Research Report 10, London 1976.

Department of the Environment, *Rural Communities: A Discussion Paper*, HMSO, London 1977.

Department of the Environment, *English House Condition Survey 1976*, HMSO, London 1978.

Department of the Environment, *Structure and Activity of the Development Industry*, Property Advisory Group, Department of the Environment, HMSO, London 1981.

Devon County Council, *County Development Plan - First Review*, Devon County Council, Devon 1964.

Devon County Council, *County Development Plan - Second Review*, Devon County Council, Devon 1972.

Devon County Council, *County Structure Plan: Report of the Survey*, Devon County Council, Devon 1977.

Devon County Council, *County Structure Plan*, Devon County Council, Devon 1979.

Donnison, D.V., *The Government of Housing*, Penguin, London 1967.

Donnison, D.V., 'Empty council houses', *Housing Review*, 28, Sept. - Oct. 1979.

Dower, M., 'Planning aspects of second homes' in Coppock, J.T. (ed.), *Second Homes: Curse or Blessing*, Pergamon, Oxford 1977.

Duncan, S., *Alienation and Explanation in Human Geography*, Discussion Paper 63, Graduate Geography School, London School of Economics, London 1977.

Dunn, M., Rawson, M. and Rogers, A., *Rural Housing: Competition and Choice*, Allen and Unwin, London 1981.

Fletcher, P., 'The control of housing standards in a rural district: a case study', *Social and Economic Administration*, 3, 1969.

Frankenberg, R., 'British community studies: problems of synthesis' in Banton, M.(ed.), *The Social Anthropology of Complex Societies*, Tavistock Publications, London 1966.

Frankenberg, R., *Communities in Britain*, Penguin, Harmondsworth 1969.

Gasson, R., *Provision of Tied Cottages*, Department of Land Economy, Working Paper No. 4 University of Cambridge, Cambridge 1975.

Gauldie, E., *Cruel Habitations: A History of Working Class Housing 1780-1918*, Allen and Unwin, London 1974.

Gilg, A.W., 'Rural employment' in Cherry, G.W. (ed.), *Rural Planning Problems*, Leonard Hill, London 1976.

Gilg, A.W., *Countryside Planning: The First Three Decades*, David and Charles, Newton Abbot 1978.

Gilg, A.W., 'Planning for rural employment in a changed economy', *The Planner*, 66, 1980a.

Gilg, A.W., *Countryside Planning Yearbook 1980*, Geo Books, Norwich 1980b.

Gilg, A.W., *Countryside Planning Yearbook 1981*, Geo Books, Norwich 1981.

Glyn-Jones, A., *Village into Town: A Study of Transition in South Devon*, Devon County Council and University of Exeter, Exeter 1977.

Glyn-Jones, A., *Rural Recovery: Has It Begun?* Devon County Council and University of Exeter, Exeter 1979.

Gray, F., 'Selection and allocation in council housing', *Transactions of the Institute of British Geographers*, New Series 1, 1976a.

Gray, F., 'The management of local authority housing' in Political Economy of Housing Workshop, *Housing and Class in Britain*, London 1976b.

Hart, J.T., 'The inverse care law', *Lancet*, 1971; also in Cox, C. and Mead, A. (eds.), *A Sociology of Medical Practice*, Collier-Macmillan, London 1975.

Harvey, D., *Social Justice and the City*, Arnold, London 1973.

Haynes, R.M., Bentham, G., Spencer, M.B. and Spratley, J.M., 'Community attitudes towards the accessibility of hospitals in West Norfolk' in Moseley, M.J. (ed.), *Social Issues in Rural Norfolk*, Centre of East Anglian Studies, University of East Anglia, Norwich 1978.

Haynes, R.M. and Bentham, C.G., *Community Hospitals and Rural Accessibility*, Saxon House, Farnborough 1979.

Heller, T., 'Health and health services' in Walker, A. (ed.), *Rural Poverty*, Poverty Pamphlet No. 37, Child Poverty Action Group, London 1978.

Heller, T., 'Rural health and health services' in Shaw, M. (ed.), *Rural Deprivation and Planning*, Geo Books, Norwich 1979.

Herbert, D.T. and Smith, D.M. (eds.), *Social Problems and the City*, Oxford University Press, Oxford 1979.

Hill, C.M., 'Leisure behaviour in six mid–Norfolk villages' in Moseley, M.J. (ed.), *Social Issues in Rural Norfolk*, Centre of East Anglian Studies, University of East Anglia, Norwich 1978.

Howe, G.M., *National Atlas of Disease Mortality in the United Kingdom*, Nelson, London 1970.

Institute of Housing, 'Housing associations, the homeless and the agricultural worker', *Housing*, 15, August 1979.

Irving, B. and Hilgendorf, L., *Tied Cottages in British Agriculture*, Working Paper No.1, The Tavistock Institute of Human Relations, London 1975.

Jacobs, C.A., *Rural Housing in Denbighshire*, Denbighshire County Council, 1974

Jones, A., *Rural Housing: The Agricultural Tied Cottage*, Occasional Papers on Social Administration No. 56, Bell, London 1975.

Jones, G.E., *Rural Life: Patterns and Processes*, Longman, London 1973.

Knox, P.L., 'The intraurban ecology of primary medical care: patterns of accessibility and their policy implications', *Environment and Planning A*, 10, 1978.

Lambert, J., Paris, C. and Blackaby, B., *Housing Policy and the State: Allocation, Access and Control,* Macmillan, London 1978.

Lansley, S., *Housing and Public Policy,* Croom Helm, London 1979.

Larkin, A., 'Inner-city infatuation – rural areas must fight it', *Municipal and Public Services Journal,* 86, 1978a.

Larkin, A., 'Rural Housing – too dear, too few and too far', *Roof,* 3, January 1978b.

Larkin, A., 'Housing and the poor' in Walker, A. (ed.), *Rural Poverty,* Poverty Pamphlet No. 37, Child Poverty Action Group, London 1978c.

Larkin, A., 'Rural housing and housing needs' in Shaw, M. (ed.), *Rural Deprivation and Planning,* Geo Books, Norwich 1979.

Law, C.M. and Warnes, A.M., 'The changing geography of the elderly in England and Wales', *Transactions of the Institute of British Geographers,* New Series 1, 1976.

Lawton, R., 'People and Work' in House, J.W. (ed.), *The UK Space,* Weidenfeld and Nicolson, London 1973.

Lewis, G.J., *Rural Communities,* David and Charles, Newton Abbot 1979.

Lewis, G.J., 'Changes and continuity in the rural community – a geographical perspective', unpublished paper presented at the Institute of British Geographers Conference, Leicester 1981.

Littlejohn, J., *Westrigg: The Sociology of a Cheviot Parish,* Routledge and Kegan Paul, London 1964.

Macey, A.E., 'Housing selection: residential qualifications and the publication of schemes', *Housing,* 16, 1980.

Martin, I., 'Rural Communities' in Cherry, G.E. (ed.), *Rural Planning Problems,* Leonard Hill, London 1976.

Moseley, M.J. (ed.), *Social Issues in Rural Norfolk,* Centre of East Anglian Studies, University of East Anglia, Norwich 1978.

Moseley, M.J., *Accessibility: The Rural Challenge,* Methuen, London 1979.

Moseley, M.J., 'Is rural deprivation really rural', *The Planner,* 66, 1980.

Nevitt, A.A., *Housing, Taxation and Subsidies: A Study of Housing in the United Kingdom,* Nelson, London 1966.

Newby, H., Bell, C., Rose, D. and Saunders, P., *Property, Paternalism and Power: Class and Control in Rural England,* Huntchinson, London 1978.

Newby, H., *Green and Pleasant Land?* Hutchinson, London 1979.

Niner, P., *Local Authority Housing Policy and Practice – a Case Study Approach,* Occasional Paper No. 31, Centre for Urban and Regional Studies, University of Birmingham, Birmingham 1975.

Orbach, L.F., *Homes for Heroes: A Study of the Evolution of British Public Housing, 1915–1921,* Seeley Service, London 1977.

Orwin, C.S., *Country Planning: A Study of Rural Problems,* Oxford Agricultural Economics Research Unit, Oxford University Press, London 1944.

Packman, J., 'Rural employment: planning and problems' in Shaw, M. (ed.), *Rural Deprivation and Planning,* Geo Books, Norwich 1979.

Pahl, R.E. (ed.), *Readings in Urban Sociology,* Pergamon, Oxford 1968.

Pahl, R.E., *Whose City?* Longmans, London 1970.

Pahl, R.E., *Whose City?* Penguin, Harmondsworth 1975.

Patmore, J.A., *Land and Leisure,* David and Charles, Newton Abbot 1970.

Phillips, D.R., 'Public attitudes to general practitioner services: a reflection of an inverse care law in intraurban primary medical care?', *Environment and Planning A,* 11, 1979.

Phillips, D.R., *Contemporary Issues in the Geography of Health Care,* Geo Books, Norwich 1981.

Phillips, D.R. and Williams, A.M., *Local Authority Housing Stock, South Hams,* South Hams Housing Project Working Paper No. 1, Exeter and Totnes 1980a.

Phillips, D.R. and Williams, A.M., *Local Authority Tenants Applications to Transfer in The South Hams,* South Hams Housing Project Working Paper No. 2, Exeter and Totnes 1980b.

Phillips, D.R. and Williams, A.M., *Housing in The South Hams: Context for Housing,* South Hams Housing Project Working Paper No. 3, Exeter and Totnes 1980c.

Phillips, D.R. and Williams, A.M., *Applications for Housing to South Hams District Council,* South Hams Housing Project Working Paper No. 4, Exeter and Totnes 1981a.

Phillips, D.R. and Williams, A.M., *Sample Tenancy Survey,* South Hams Housing Project Working Paper No. 5, Exeter and Totnes 1981b.

Pinch, S.P., 'Patterns of local authority housing allocation in Greater London between 1966 and 1973: an inter-borough analysis', *Transactions of the Institute of British Geographers,* New Series 3, 1978.

Pinch, S.P., 'Territorial justice in the city: a case study of the social services for the elderly in Greater London' in Herbert, D.T. and Smith, D.M. (eds.), *Social Problems and the City,* Oxford University Press, Oxford 1979.

Pinch, S.P., 'Local authority provision for the elderly: an overview and case study of London' in Herbert, D.T. and Johnston, R.J. (eds.), *Geography and the Urban Environment,* Vol. III, Wiley, London 1980.

Popplestone, G., 'Difficult tenants: who they are and what to do about them', *Centre for Environmental Studies Review,* January 1979.

Rex, J. and Moore, R., *Race, Community and Conflict,* Oxford University Press, London 1967.

Robson, B.T., 'Housing, empiricism and the state' in Herbert, D.T. and Smith, D.M. (eds.), *Social Problems and the City,* Oxford University Press, Oxford 1979.

Rogers, A.W., 'Rural housing' in Cherry, G. (ed.), *Rural Planning Problems,* Leonard Hill, London 1976.

Rose, D., Saunders, P., Newby, H. and Bell, C., 'Landownership and the politics of rural areas' in Walker, A. (ed.), *Rural Poverty,* Poverty Pamphlet No. 37, Child Poverty Action Group, London 1978.

Rose, D., Saunders, P., Newby, H. and Bell, C., 'The economic and political basis of rural deprivation: a case study' in Shaw, M. (ed.), *Rural Deprivation and Planning,* Geo Books, Norwich 1979.

Rossi, P.H., *Why Families Move,* Free Press of Glencoe, New York 1955.

Sarre, P., *Second Homes,* A Guided Project Course in Human Geography, Module 2, Open University Press, Milton Keynes 1981.

Saville, J., *Rural Depopulation in England and Wales, 1851-1951,* Routledge and Kegan Paul, London 1957.

Schifferes, S., 'Housing Bill 1980: the beginning of the end for council housing', *Roof,* 5, 1980a.

Schifferes, S., 'New mobility moves', *Roof,* 5, 1980b.

Schifferes, S., 'Tied accommodation: letting without strings', *Housing and Planning Review,* 36, 1980c.

Shaw, G. and Toyne, P., 'Manpower demands, labour supplies and employment aspirations: a problem with implications for the formulation of regional policy', *Geoforum*, 9, 1978.

Shaw, G. and Williams, A., 'The regional structure of structure plans', *Planning Outlook*, 23, 1980.

Shaw, M., (ed.), *Rural Deprivation and Planning*, Geo Books, Norwich, 1979a.

Shaw, M., 'Rural deprivation and social planning: an overview' in Shaw, M. (ed.), *Rural Deprivation and Planning*, Geo Books, Norwich 1979b.

Shelter, *Caravans in Bordon*, Shelter, 1970.

Shucksmith, M., *No Homes for Locals*, Gower, Farnborough 1981.

Smith, D.M., *Human Geography: A Welfare Approach*, Edward Arnold, London 1977.

Smith, D.M., *Where the Grass is Greener*, Penguin, Harmondsworth 1979.

South West Economic Planning Council, *Survey of Second Homes in the South West*, HMSO, London 1975.

Stacey, M., *Tradition and Change: A Study of Banbury*, Oxford University Press, Oxford 1960.

Stamp, L.D., 'The planning of land use', *The Advancement of Science*, 6, 1949.

Stockford, D., 'Social services provision in rural Norfolk' in Moseley, M.J. (ed.), *Social Issues in Rural Norfolk*, Centre of East Anglian Studies, University of East Anglia, Norwich 1978.

Taylor, G. and Ayres, N., *Born and Bred Unequal*, Longman, London 1970.

Taylor, P.J., ' "Difficult-to-let", "difficult-to-live-in", and sometimes "difficult-to-get-out-of": an essay on the provision of council housing, with special reference to Killingworth', *Environment and Planning A*, 11, 1979.

Thomas, C. and Winyard, S., 'Rural incomes' in Shaw, M. (ed.), *Rural Deprivation and Planning*, Geo Books, Norwich 1979.

Vane, R. de., *Second Home Ownership: A Case Study*, Bangor Occasional Papers in Economics No. 6, University of Wales Press, Cardiff 1975.

Ventris, N., 'Recreational and cultural provision in rural areas' in Shaw, J.M. (ed.), *Rural Deprivation and Planning*, Geo Books, Norwich 1979.

171

Walker, A., 'Introduction and background' in Walker, A. (ed.), *Rural Poverty*, Poverty Pamphlet No. 37, Child Poverty Action Group, London 1978a.

Walker, A. (ed.), *Rural Poverty*, Poverty Pamphlet No. 37, Child Poverty Action Group, London 1978b.

Watkins, R., 'Deprivation and education in rural schools' in Walker, A. (ed.), *Rural Poverty*, Poverty Pamphlet No. 37, Child Poverty Action Group, London 1978.

Watkins, R., 'Educational disadvantage in rural areas' in Shaw, M. (ed.), *Rural Deprivation and Planning*, Geo Books, Norwich 1979.

Watson, C., 'Sale of council houses: the right to buy-policy implications', *Housing Review*, 29, 1980.

Watson, C., Forrest, R., Groves, R., Jarman, R. and Williams, P., 'Housing investment programmes and the private sector', *Local Government Studies*, 6, 1979.

Weightman, G., 'The making of modern slum estates', *New Society*, 29 June 1978.

While, A.E., 'The vital role of the cottage-community hospital', *Journal of the Royal College of General Practitioners*, 28, 1978.

Williams, P.R., 'The role of institutions in the Inner London housing market', *Transactions of the Institute of British Geographers*, New Series 1, 1976.

Williams, W.M., *The Sociology of an English Village: Gosforth*, Routledge and Kegan Paul, London 1956.

Winyard, S., 'Low pay and farmworkers' in Walker, A. (ed.), *Rural Poverty*, Poverty Pamphlet No. 37, Child Poverty Action Group, London 1978a.

Winyard, S., 'Points to a good policy', *Roof*, 3, 1978b.

Woodruffe, B.J., *Rural Settlement Policies and Plans*, Oxford University Press, London 1976.

Index

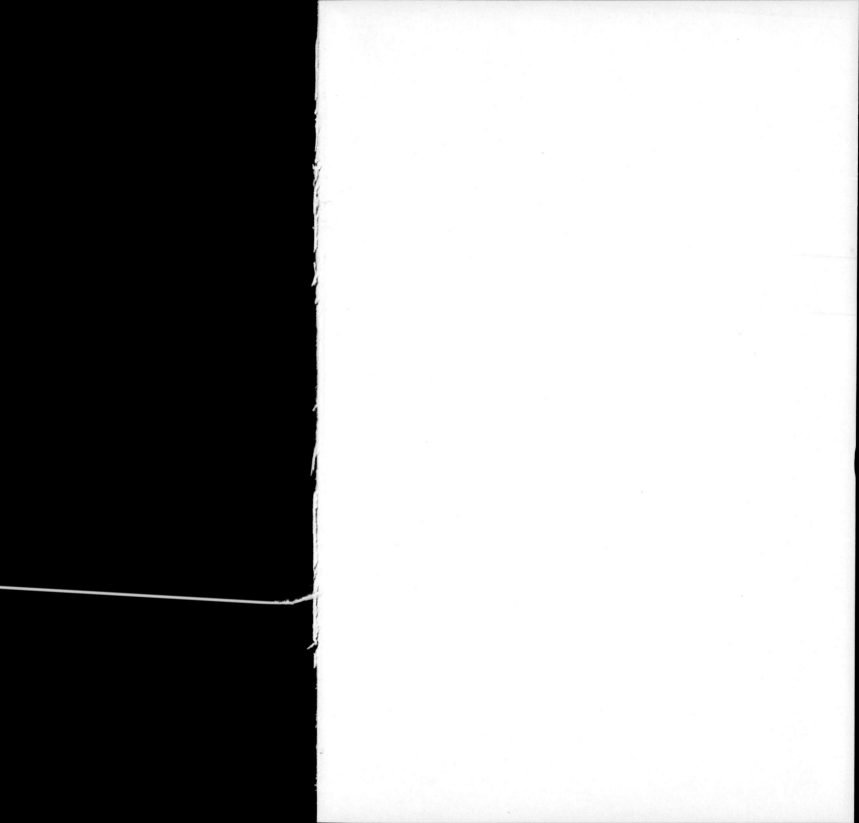